THE CIRCUS
AND OTHER ESSAYS
AND FUGITIVE PIECES

JOYCE KILMER

THE CIRCUS

AND OTHER ESSAYS
AND FUGITIVE PIECES

BY

JOYCE KILMER

EDITED WITH INTRODUCTION BY
ROBERT CORTES HOLLIDAY

KENNIKAT PRESS, INC./PORT WASHINGTON, N. Y.

THE CIRCUS AND OTHER ESSAYS AND FUGITIVE PIECES

Copyright 1921 by George H. Doran Company
Reissued 1968 by Kennikat Press
By arrangement with Doubleday & Company, Inc.

Library of Congress Catalog Card No: 68-26250
Manufactured in the United States of America

ESSAY AND GENERAL LITERATURE INDEX REPRINT SERIES

TO

ALINE KILMER

ACKNOWLEDGMENTS

Credit is gratefully accorded the *New York Times, America, Contemporary Verse,* and *Poetry: A Magazine of Verse,* for permission to reprint several of the pieces collected in this volume. For the privilege of reprinting poems quoted by Kilmer in his articles and lectures, acknowledgment is made to the following publishers: E. P. Dutton & Company, Dodd, Mead and Company, Charles Scribner's Sons, John Lane Company, The Macmillan Company, Methuen and Company, Boni and Liveright, and Burns and Oates. And the permission of George Sterling is greatly appreciated for the right to reproduce his three sonnets on Oblivion. The article on Thomas Hardy, prepared as the Introduction to the Modern Library Edition of "The Mayor of Casterbridge," is reproduced by special arrangement with Boni and Liveright. The publishers of "Warner's Library of the World's Best Literature" have courteously extended permission to reprint here the four essays, originally written for that work, which conclude this volume.

R. C. H.

New York, 1921.

CONTENTS

PAGE

INTRODUCTION BY ROBERT CORTES HOLLIDAY..... 13

THE CIRCUS, AND OTHER ESSAYS

THE CIRCUS.................................... 45
THE ABOLITION OF POETS...................... 60
NOON-HOUR ADVENTURING...................... 70
SIGNS AND SYMBOLS............................ 83
THE GREAT NICKEL ADVENTURE................. 88
THE URBAN CHANTICLEER...................... 96
DAILY TRAVELING............................. 105
INCONGRUOUS NEW YORK....................... 110
IN MEMORIAM: JOHN BUNNY.................... 116
THE DAY AFTER CHRISTMAS.................... 125

FUGITIVE PIECES

THE ASHMAN................................. 137
THE BEAR THAT WALKS LIKE A MAN............ 146
ABSINTHE AT THE CHESHIRE CHEESE........... 153
JAPANESE LACQUER........................... 159
SAPPHO REDIVIVA............................ 168
THE POETRY OF GERARD HOPKINS.............. 180
PHILOSOPHICAL TENDENCIES IN ENGLISH LITERATURE 186
TWO LECTURES ON ENGLISH POETRY:
    THE BALLAD............................. 197
    THE SONNET............................. 203
GILBERT K. CHESTERTON AND HIS POETRY........ 222

ix

PAGE

LIONEL JOHNSON, ERNEST DOWSON, AUBREY BEARDS-
  LEY 237
SWINBURNE AND FRANCIS THOMPSON............ 253
A NOTE ON THOMAS HARDY.................. 268
MADISON JULIUS CAWEIN..................... 275
FRANCIS THOMPSON......................... 282
JOHN MASEFIELD........................... 288
WILLIAM VAUGHN MOODY.................... 302

INTRODUCTION

INTRODUCTION

I

SINCE last I took up my pen in the service of my friend who on July 30, 1918, laid down his sword in the service of his country, fame, and yet greater fame, has been busy with his name. Any further eulogy by my hand would have only the point of being altogether superfluous and the foolish effect of being very much at the rear of the situation. Further, the story of Joyce Kilmer, doubtless in very fair measure, is known to nearly everyone. An account of his career is not to be appreciably elaborated here.

There are, however, some facts in explanation of the appearance of this volume at this time which require to be set down. And a number of circumstances in relation to the material here collected may be told, I think, to general interest. With these matters I am probably as familiar as anyone, and so have the great privilege of undertaking to record them.

INTRODUCTION

The ten highly humorous and altogether charming essays which form the first part of this volume have led a rather queer life so far—though I think their existence will be a very happy one from now on. First, they were not "essays" at the time of their birth. They came into the world as "articles." So they were spoken of by the young journalist who at various times and with very little to do about the matter wrote them in the course of a bewildering variety of other activities. Or, to be still more frank, he was perhaps more apt to refer to them, when he did refer to them at all, as "Sunday stories," done as a part of his job with the *New York Times Sunday Magazine*. What they were called, however, is neither here nor there. The thing is that they are here.

At the time they were offered for book publication their author, then about thirty years of age, was well established as the author of "Trees and Other Poems"—poems which had been appearing for some time in various publications, collected and issued in book form in 1914. He had been for several years a conspicuous figure and an invaluable worker in the Poetry Society of America and the Dickens Fellowship. He was a member of the Authors Club, and several other organizations. He had been a lexicographer and an associate magazine editor. He was a "star" book reviewer, conducted the Poetry Department of *The Literary Digest,* associated much with literary celebrities, and appeared in *Who's Who.* The point I am getting at is that he had a good deal of what is called a "name."

Satan finds mischief for idle hands to do. I suppose that is why the thought occurred to Joyce to get out a book of prose. So, as the professional literary term has it, he "pasted up" ten of his articles—that is, cut them out of the newspaper and stuck them column width down the middle of sheets of "copy" paper. He typed a title page, "The Circus and Other Essays," and submitted his manuscript to a publisher. It was promptly "turned down." Joyce again did up his manuscript, gummed on some fresh stamps, and again away it went to another leading publishing house. And—well, and so on. I do not know precisely how many times this manuscript was submitted for publication; but I know it was a number, a good number, of times.

That, however, "The Circus" seemed likely not to find any publisher at all at that time is not a matter for anything like astonishment. Not when one bears in mind a publishing hobgoblin of the day. The book was labeled "essays" and therefore damned. And here, perhaps, it may not be too irrelevant to take a brief glance at the whole history of this mysterious thing, the light, familiar essay in English. In the Augustan age of English prose, we remember, appeared the easy, graceful style of Steele and Addison, so admirably suited to the pleasant narrative form of essay which they introduced. And in the nineteenth century in England, when Johnson and Goldsmith were followed by Lamb, Hazlitt, De Quincey, Leigh Hunt, Macaulay, Carlyle, Ruskin and all the rest, the essay certainly appears to have been, so to say, very much the go.

Irving, Emerson, Thoreau, Hawthorne, Lowell, Holmes—certainly our fathers were not afraid of essays. Nevertheless, somewhere about the opening of our own day an iron-bound tradition became erected in the publishing business, at least in the United States, that books of essays would not sell; could not be made to sell even sufficiently to avoid a considerable loss on the investment of manufacture; in fact, were quite impossible as a publishing venture. No matter how much a publisher himself, or his manuscript reader, might enjoy a col-

INTRODUCTION

lection of essays that chanced to turn up in his shop, his conviction as to its unmarketability as a book was not altered—not even stirred. A few, a very few, essayists there were, indeed, who got published. Agnes Repplier and Samuel McChord Crothers most prominent, perhaps, among them. But these writers had somehow got established as essayists. They were found on the lists only of a house with peculiarly "literary" traditions, which it was business policy to capitalize and perpetuate for the sake of the firm's "imprint." I have heard scoffers among publishers ask if "anybody outside of New England" bought the books of these writers. Maybe their prime function was, in the publishing term, to "dress the list." The volumes of essays by Dr. Henry van Dyke, I know from experience as a bookseller, sold in popular measure. And now and then a volume of collected papers by, say, Meredith Nicholson would bob up for a short space of time. But such instances as these did not affect the general situation.

In general, when the manuscript of "The Circus" was "going the rounds" it was (supposedly) economic madness, at any rate professional heresy, not to regard books of essays as what the trade terms "plugs," and a drug on the market. Doubtless, the publishing position in this matter was evolved from cumulative facts of experience in the past. But a screw was loose somewhere. The publishing barometer had, it would seem, failed to note a change in the weather of the public mind.

That "The Circus" would not have made a fairly popular book at the time it was first submitted for publication, it seems to me, there is a good deal of reason to believe was a fallacy. Not a couple of years afterward a collection of random articles in general character not dissimilar to "The Circus," by another young man of greatly likable nature, but then practically unknown outside the circle of his personal friends, was in some idiosyncratic moment accepted, and directly won its way to a very considerable sale and a very fair degree of fame. About then, too, along came another book of pasted-up "papers" (about which I happen to know a good deal), which after having been rejected by nearly every publishing house in America was taken in a spirit of generous friendliness by a publisher of much enterprise, began almost at once to sell as well as a fairly successful novel, has been numerous times reprinted, and in the way of luck brought its altogether obscure author something of a name. And just now the light, personal, journalistic-literary essay is having quite a brisk vogue.

If Joyce stood to-day merely where he stood five years ago "The Circus," without doubt, would be snapped up by anybody. More; some publisher's "scout" very likely would get a "hunch" about the probability of Joyce's having sufficient material in his scrap-book for such a volume and "go after" it even before Joyce had submitted it to the house of this fellow's connection. But, alas! for "ifs" and "might have beens." Fair fortune did not attend "The Circus."

Failing of placing the book with any large house having an extensive and organized machinery for carrying it to a wide audience, Joyce welcomed the opportunity of having the book published by his friend Laurence J. Gomme. Mr. Gomme had been for several years the proprietor of the Little Book Shop Around the Corner, at number two East Twenty-ninth Street, directly across the street from the Protestant Episcopal Church of the Transfiguration, so altogether charming in its Old World effect, nestling in a tiny green spot hemmed in by high buildings, and known to fame and legend as the Little Church Around the Corner. This was a shop conducted in excellent taste, a sort of salon for pleasant persons of literary breeding, and its "circulars" were written by no less an advertising man than Richard Le Gallienne. In addition to selling the best books of other publishers, Mr. Gomme (at a good deal of risk to himself) served the cause of good literature by himself issuing now and then a volume of a nature close to his heart.

In the autumn of 1916 he published, in a very attractive form, the American edition of Mr. Belloc's poems. The volume was entitled "Verses," by Hilaire Belloc. The introduction to the book by Kilmer was reprinted in the two volume set, "Joyce Kilmer: Poems, Essays and Letters," under the title "The Poetry of Hilaire Belloc." That same fall Mr. Gomme published "The Circus and Other Essays." He made a charming little book: a thin volume in size betwixt and between what the book trade calls a "16mo" volume and a duodecimo; bound in plain tan boards, with olive cloth back stamped in gold; very neatly printed on soft cream paper in rather small type. The book had a rather fantastically amusing and somewhat lurid "jacket," picturing in black and yellow the professional activities of several clowns.

A very pleasant bibelot, but, I felt then, not a volume effective in catching the popular trade. For one thing, it looked very much like it might be a book of verse. Also, the book was so thin that one would not be likely to catch sight of it standing among other volumes in a row on a bookstore shelf.

Mr. Gomme's means as a publisher at that time did not permit him to give the book any paid advertising; it had no campaign whatever of free publicity behind it. Nor had the publisher any traveling salesmen to show the book to dealers over the country. He merely "covered" New York City himself in the interests of the volumes he issued. Indeed, one would not be making a hilarious exaggeration in saying that "The Circus" was semi-"privately printed."

A fair number of copies of the book were sent out for review. And here is a very interesting thing. The book, as has been said, was decidedly insignificant in bulk. It was published at a time when the assumption prevailed that there was no appreciable public for volumes of essays; and consequently, the inference would be, the publication of such a book was quite without news value. Further, it was issued at a period when newsprint paper was appallingly scarce, newspaper space rigorously conserved, and the war engrossing public attention. There was, too, as we have seen, nothing about the

launching of "The Circus" to tempt any literary
editor or reviewer to believe that the book was of
any consequence whatever. Indeed, half a "stick"
of fairly favorable comment here and there would
have been all that anybody could reasonably have
expected in the way of a "press." But, as a matter of fact, all in all the book got a surprising
amount of space in the papers, and was awarded
the dignity of thoughtful appreciation. The *New
York Evening Post* devoted half the front page of
its book review section to an article, which was continued through a column of another page, to "The
Circus" and another book of essays with which it
was grouped.

Shortly after the publication of "The Circus" the
difficulties of the business of bookselling and publishing at this time forced Mr. Gomme to close out
his business. And for a period his affairs were
very much involved. His stock in hand was scattered, and before long his recent publications became exceedingly difficult to obtain. A couple of
years after the date of its imprint, Mr. Belloc, in
the course of correspondence which I had with him
mainly relating to other matters, repeatedly be-
sought me to obtain for him a copy of his "Verses,"
the volume containing Kilmer's introduction. In-

deed, he was apparently much put out by the fact that, as he expressed it, he had never even seen a copy of the American edition of his poems. I had more than a little difficulty in finding a copy to send to him. This he never received. With some petulance he laid its loss to the German submarines, which he declared sank everything that was being sent to him. I found the trail to another copy of "Verses" still more elusive; and, to tell the truth, I really don't know whether or not I got another copy off to him. This story is to show that anyone who has a copy of that book now has a volume far from readily found.

Copies of the original edition of "The Circus" are somewhat easier to lay hold of. Doubtless, though, they will soon be scarce, as the original edition could not have been large. And the book will not be reprinted in its first form. With all the untoward circumstances of its publication, however, "The Circus" did seem to find its way to no mean circle of friends. When the memorial volumes, "Joyce Kilmer: Poems, Essays and Letters," were published in the autumn of 1918, numerous inquiries were received by the publishers as to why the essays which comprised the volume "The Circus" were not included. The explanation is this: In the continuance of the entanglement of the affairs of Mr. Gomme's former business no clear title to the rights of this book was at that time in sight. Since then these matters have all been straightened out, and, I am happy to be able to say, this excellent friend of Joyce Kilmer is again in circumstances more auspicious than before, and with joy to his fine heart, effectively serving the cause of good books.

In direct critical appreciation of these ten essays there is not much that I care to say. They were written by my friend, and are therefore holy. That is, of course, to me. They may be charged with being very youthful. Aye; even so.

> For ever warm and still to be enjoy'd,
>   For ever panting and for ever young.

Their youthfulness is to me a thing of very poignant, tender beauty. I see again that radiant boy, trailing clouds of glory come from God who was his home. His childhood spent in "a town less than a hundred miles from New York," "now he feels himself actually a New Yorker," "enjoys the proud novelty of working for wages," and "joyfully, therefore, he goes forth every noon to explore the

territory of his new possession." The subway was
to him "the great nickel adventure"; a ride on the
elevated railroad, "aërial journeying"; his alarm
clock, "the urban chanticleer." Again, as a commuter, I see him on the 5.24, flying across "leagues"
to his cottage in the "primeval forest" of New Jersey. On his "red velvet chair" he sits, "enjoying
with his neighbors tobacco smoke, rapid travel, and
the news of the world." None ever enjoyed these
things more, red velvet chair and all!

The connection which I may boast of having
with the writing of some of these essays illustrates
in an amusing way the pleasantly pugnacious character of Joyce's mind. Joyce held that I was offensively æsthetic in regarding sign-boards about
the countryside as ugly things. "Signs and Symbols" was his hilarious and scornful rebuke. "The
Gentle Art of Christmas Giving" (a *New York
Times* article reprinted in the two-volume set) had
a similar origin. You remember with what amusing gusto it begins:

If a dentist stuck a bit of holly in his cap and
went through the streets on Christmas morning, his
buzzing drill over his shoulder and his forceps in
his hand, stopping at the houses of his friends to
give their jaws free treatment, meanwhile trolling

out lusty Yuletide staves—if he were to do this, I say, it would be said of him, among other things, that he was celebrating Christmas in a highly original manner. Undoubtedly there would be many other adjectives applied to his manner of generosity —adjectives applied, for instance, by the children whom, around their gayly festooned tree, he surprised with his gift of expert treatment. But the adjective most generally used (not perhaps in adulation) would be "original." And the use of this adjective would be utterly wrong.

The holly-bedecked dentist would not be acting in the original manner. He would be following the suggestion of his own philanthropic heart. He would be acting in accordance with tradition, a particularly annoying tradition, the evil and absurd superstition that a gift should be representative of the giver rather than of the recipient.

That "particularly annoying tradition," that "evil and absurd superstition," I had been guilty of voicing a few days before he wrote this article. He looked at me with withering commiseration.

If, in the days when he was writing the essays of "The Circus," Joyce had the effect of being ridiculously young, he was also (with affection I say it) ridiculously wise for his years. I can hear the sturdy sound of his voice in the phrase (in the essay "The Abolition of Poets"), "those ridiculous young people who call themselves Imagists and Vorticists and similar queer names." And what joyous satire here:

And there is Zipp, the What-is-it? most venerable of freaks, whose browless tufted head and amazing figure have entertained his visitors since Phineas Taylor Barnum engaged him to ornament his museum on Ann Street. For all I know, Zipp is a poet—his smile is lyrical, and in his roving eyes there is a suggestion of vers libre.

Then, with the mellow humor of paternal experience he discusses (in "The Day After Christmas") that hypothetical person who is three, and who, he regrets to say, is "somewhat sticky"; who, further, had in all confidence requested Santa Claus to bring him a large live baboon, but who had been brought instead a small tin monkey on a stick. Or, again, babies who at somewhere between six and eight in the morning, "seeing that their weary parents are leaving them, decide at last that it is time to go to sleep."

And even then, as throughout his later years, he had that (manly not sentimental) intuitive sympathy for those by fortune afflicted. In "The Circus":

INTRODUCTION

The freaks get large salaries (they seem large to poets), and they are carefully tended, for they are delicate. See, here is a man who lives although his back is broken. There is a crowd around him; how interested they are! Would they be as interested in a poet who lived although his heart was broken? Probably not. But then, there are not many freaks.

Nor did his perception of sorrow come to him solely by intuition. Far from it. No, this very valiant and very young man himself had experienced the fact that an alarm clock "can utter harsh and strident grief, those know who lie down with Sorrow and must awaken with her."

To me there is something indescribably touching even in Joyce's most hilarious flights of fancy in these essays. I cannot tell you why this is so. Perhaps it is because his jocund humor, like all else, sprang from a heart so woven of the common strands of humanity.

When Adam watched with pleased astonishment an agile monkey leap among the branches of an Eden tree, and laughed at the foolish face of a giraffe, he saw a circus. Delightedly now would he sit upon a rickety chair beneath a canvas roof, smell the romantic aroma of elephant and trampled grass, and look at wonders.

INTRODUCTION

The most obvious thing, of course, about these essays is their Chestertonian spirit and manner. In the matter of the manner, Mr. Chesterton's trick of "reverse English," to employ the billiard player's term, take this:

It would be the mere prose of our daily life for birds to fly about close to the tent's roof, and for men and women to ring bells and sit in rocking chairs. It is the poetry of the circus that men and women fly about close to the tent's roof, and birds ring bells and sit in rocking chairs.

Or, for both manner and spirit, this:

By faith the walls of Jericho fell down. By faith the Eight Algerian Aërial Equilibrists stayed up.

Indeed, the whole fundamental temper of the book —its glorification (almost deification) of everyday things; its militant persistence in running counter to dull acceptance of current ideas; its sleight-of-hand dexterity in bringing a thing to life by standing it on its head—is Chestertonian. And right there is the point. Anybody, almost, can copy, or parody, Mr. Chesterton's manner. But Kilmer's Chestertonism was nothing of a superficial imitation. He was at heart quite Chestertonian himself.

What is still more to the point: He was, so to put it, more Chestertonian than even Mr. Chesterton. That is, one cannot but feel that for some considerable time Mr. Chesterton has been more or less mechanically imitating himself. But Kilmer's rollicking pages have on them the tender bloom of the natural fruit.

And they reek with the articles of his creed—are punctuated with the touchstones by which he guided his life. Three words are most often repeated in these essays. They occur again and again, one or more of them on nearly every page. These words, you cannot fail to note, are: faith, mirth, and democracy.

II

The poem, "The Ashman," which opens the second part of this book, was not included in the collected set of Kilmer's poems, essays and letters for the reason that it was overlooked at the time those volumes were being prepared for publication. The poem was supplied for this volume by Charles Wharton Stork, in whose magazine, "Contemporary Verse," it originally appeared.

Among Kilmer's papers I have found a typewritten memorandum which shows that he contem-

Raphaelite Brotherhood and Their Successors."
This is, I think, a better lecture than "Swinburne
and Francis Thompson." It is an attempt to show
how Patmore (who was a member of the Pre-Raphaelite Brotherhood, a friend of Rossetti and a con-
tributor to The Germ) carried the theories of the
Pre-Raphaelites to their logical conclusion, that
Rossetti and Christina and Morris and a lot of that
bunch really paved the way for Francis Thompson
and Alice Meynell and Katherine Tynan and other
modern Catholic poets, by writing sympathetically,
even if not always understandingly, on Catholic
themes. Incidentally, I trace "The Hound of
Heaven" back through "The Blessed Damozel" to
"The Raven." But if you don't want that lecture
I'll lecture on any other subject you may elect—
the lighter lyrics of James J. Daly, for example.

In another letter he writes: "Next year I won't
lecture at all; I'll just recite my poems, which take
better than the lectures, anyway. I'm going on
tour with Ellis Parker Butler, the 'Pigs Is Pigs'
man, and we'll have a regular manager."

And again:

I am glad that you are so forgiving as to be
willing to have me at Campion on the twenty-sixth.
Unless I am commanded to the contrary, I will
give "The War and the Poets" at the College and

INTRODUCTION

"Francis Thompson" at the Convent. "The War and the Poets" does not get the goats of hyphenates of any sort—I gave it in Toronto and in Notre Dame. Also I will read some of my own stuff, new and old, at both of these lectures unless forcibly prevented.

The two lectures on poetry, "The Ballad" and "The Sonnet," were given at New York University, and were to have been parts of a book on the art of versification, which the University, I believe, was to publish. In the manuscript of these lectures we find such phrases as "this book," and Joyce referring to himself here as "the author of a textbook." The lecture "The Ballad" as here printed is incomplete, as the typewritten copy of the manuscript which came into my hands, and which is the only copy I know to be in existence, ends thus:

I will call the reader's attention to the work of some of the poets who, in our time, have been proving the falsity of Sir Arthur Quiller-Couch's statement that

These lectures on poetry are admirably adapted to their end. They are addressed to the student, especially "the apprentices of the craft of verse making." They are devoted altogether to historical and technical matters. And in the earnestness of his conception of his task here as the author of a textbook, Joyce has very rigorously excluded anything which could possibly be fancied as flippant. Just as sternly has he refrained from allowing to enter his discourse any particle of color of religious bias. He has not, however, in the slightest permitted his independence of judgment to be subdued in his interpretation of purely literary points. So these lectures do not lack for vitality, and exhibit again, in a less known manner of his writing, his exceptional clarity of style.

As in his life, so in his writings. Joyce moved in many circles, and though always quite himself, so did he, too, always fit where he found himself. An exceedingly active professional writer, he was called upon to write for various audiences. When he was entrusted with writing the articles on Madison Cawein, Francis Thompson, John Masefield, and William Vaughn Moody for "Warner's Library of the World's Best Literature," and when he was invited to contribute the introductory essay to Thomas Hardy's novel "The Mayor of Casterbridge" in "The Modern Library," he was to address a more or less popular audience of general character, and he did that with ability and distinguished literary tact.

Naturally, Joyce became much in demand as a speaker before purely Catholic audiences. And naturally before Roman Catholic schools, colleges, universities and societies he loosed the spirit of his own fervent Catholicism. Perhaps it will occur to some readers of this volume who may not be Catholics that such lectures as "Lionel Johnson, Ernest Dowson, Aubrey Beardsley" and "Swinburne and Francis Thompson" are more in the nature of briefs for the Catholic Faith than they are of the character of disinterested literary criticism. I do not think it would have worried Joyce to have been told so. He was in such lectures talking what was to him far more than literature. In a letter of his before me, written by hand, he says, "There are in the universe only two ecstasies. One is receiving Holy Communion." The other, he means, is his love for his wife. "Poetry," he continues, "is not an ecstasy, but it is a delight, a shadow and an echo of the two ecstasies. It certainly is a delight to read and to make."

What, to his mind, was the use of writers, anyway? In the lecture "Philosophical Tendencies in

English Literature" he tells very definitely his conviction as to this:

So writers may fulfill the purpose for which they were made by writing—may know God better by writing about Him, increase their love of Him by expressing it in beautiful words, serve Him in this world by means of their best talent, and because of this service and His mercy be happy with Him forever in Heaven.

III

Numerous letters written by Joyce to many of his friends, and kindly loaned by their owners to the publishers, were received too late for inclusion in the two-volume set of his poems, essays and letters. These letters continue in greater detail, and give the emphasis of cumulative effect, to the portrait of a beautiful and a joyous young manhood revealed by the letters which were printed. A man has only one life to live in this world, but (if he is anything like Kilmer) many friends. And so it is that several groups of letters from his hand are more than apt to tell, with some variations in expression, very much the same story. Two stout volumes of collected letters sometimes are compiled as an appropriate part of the literary remains of a notable life. Anything approaching such a bulk of preserved correspondence, however, can only be in order when that life has reflected something like three or four times the number of working years that were Kilmer's.

Some few points I find in the unpublished letters which may be new to many of Joyce's readers. In one place he says, referring to the approaching publication of the volume which was issued as "Trees and Other Poems," "My Book is to appear next October. It is called 'The Twelve-forty-five and Other Poems.'" A little later he writes:

I wish you'd suggest a name for my book. In my contract it is called "Trees and Other Poems" but I don't like that; it's too mild. I wanted to call it "Delicatessen," since it contains a long poem of that name, but the publishers think that name too frivolous. Then I suggested "A Rumbling Wain" (after the third and fourth lines of the first stanza of Patmore's "Angel in the House") but that's too obscure. And "The 12.45 and Other Poems" is flat, I think. If you select a title, you see, you can't roast the title when you review the book in *America!*

In another place: "I don't like the book's jacket at all. I think it is effeminate."

INTRODUCTION

As an amusingly frank comment on his own "stuff" there is this:

My article in ———— was somewhat weak-minded. Have poor Christmas poem in ————
and good Christmas poem ($50.00!!) in ————.
And middling Thanksgiving poem in ————.
And trite but amiable poem about English university at war in ————.

Of Chesterton he has this very quotable line, "He is the plumed knight of literature with the sword of wit and burnished shield of Faith." All about, of course, is the Kilmerian humor. He asks his wife to, "Remember me to your new young infant Christopher." He says to a friend, "I'm sending you some postcards. The person not Mike in the picture was Mike's mother." And again:

Will you please tell me at your earliest convenience the name of an asylum for blind orphans, or something of the sort, which wants picture-postcards? I have a truckful of them, and there's no room in the house for them and us, and yet I don't want to throw them away.

Occasionally he speaks of Rose, his little daughter afflicted with infantile paralysis: "Rose is in good general health and spirits, thank God. She can use one fore-arm a little. But I cannot talk much about her, except to Our Lady." Over and over again, he says (ridiculously enough), that he is much worried about his work, he is "disgustingly lazy." And always he asked his friends to pray for him. He speaks of Father Corbet:

He ran the retreat last week. I got my soul scraped pretty clean, but it soils easily.

Remember me to everyone, and please pray very hard for,

Your affectionate friend.

IV

In the Memoir prefixed to the two-volume set are a couple of errors of fact. As a matter of record these should be corrected. The Memoir reads:

Kilmer was graduated from Rutgers College in 1904, and received his A.B. from Columbia in 1906. . . . As a Sophomore Kilmer became engaged to Miss Aline Murray. . . . Upon leaving Columbia he . . . returned to New Jersey and began his career as instructor of Latin at Morristown High School. . . . He married and became a householder.

Kilmer never graduated from Rutgers College. He graduated from Rutgers Preparatory School

INTRODUCTION

in 1904. He went to Rutgers College for two years, finishing his Sophomore year. His Junior and Senior years were at Columbia University. He graduated from there in 1908. Two weeks after his graduation he married.

The date of Kilmer's death has not been exactly established. The Memoir states, "Sergeant Kilmer was killed in action near the Ourcq, July 30, 1918." The date popularly accepted is Sunday, July 28. It was at the dawn of this day that the 165th made its gallant and irresistible drive into the five days' battle which followed. The Government telegram to Joyce's widow gave the date of his death as August 1, as does also his death certificate. His Citation for valor, however, names the date as July 30.

At the time the Memoir was written Joyce was buried near where he had fallen, perhaps ten minutes' walk to the south of the village of Seringes. Later his body was removed to a cemetery. This cemetery is 608 at Seringes et Nesles, in the Province of Aisne. It is within walking distance of a little village, Fere en Tardenois. The cemetery is a small one. It is described as being in a beautiful location, on a little elevation close by the road. The place is about ninety miles from Paris.

THE CIRCUS AND OTHER ESSAYS

THE CIRCUS

I

RESTRAINT is perhaps the most conspicuous literary virtue of the artists in words who have the pleasant task of describing in programs, in newspaper advertisements, and on posters the excellences of circuses. The litterateur who, possessed of an intimate knowledge of the circus, merely calls it "a new, stupendous, dazzling, magnificent, spectacular, educational, and awe-inspiring conglomeration of marvels, mysteries, mirth, and magic," deserves praise for a verbal economy almost Greek. For he is not verbose and extravagant, he is taciturn and thrifty; he deliberately uses the mildest instead of the strongest of the adjectives at his disposal.

Shyly, it seems, but in fact artfully, he uses modest terms—"new," for example, and "spectacular" and "educational." These are not necessarily words of praise. An epidemic may be new, an earthquake may be spectacular, and even a session of school may be educational. Yet the adjectives

proper to these catastrophes are actually applied
—in letters of gold and silver and purple—to the
circus!

The laureate of the circus, with an æsthetic
shrewdness which places him at once on a level with
Walter Pater (whose description of the "Mona
Lisa," by the by, is an admirable example of Circus
press-agent writing) considers, and rejects as too
bewilderingly true, the mightiest of the adjectives
that fit his theme. Discreetly he calls it "new" instead of "immemorial"; "educational" instead of
"religious." He does not, as he might, call the
circus poetic, he does not call it aristocratic, he does
not call it democratic. Yet all these great words
are, as he well knows, his to use. The consciousness
of his power makes him gentle.

His abnegation becomes the more startlingly virtuous when it is considered that he resists the temptation to use that fascinating device, paradox. For
the circus is paradox itself—this reactionary and
futuristic exhibition, full of Roman chariots and
motor cycles, of high romance and grotesque realism, this demonstration of democracy and aristocracy, equality and subordination, worldliness and
religion.

The press agent may, without fear of logical contradiction, call the circus religious. In the old days, he frequently called it a "moral exhibition." This was to forestall or answer the attacks of the Puritan divines of New England, who railed against the great canvas monster which invaded the sanctity of their villages.

"Moral" was justly used. For surely courage, patience, and industry are the three qualities most obviously exhibited by the silk-and-spangle clad men and women who dance on the perilous wire, fly through space on swiftly swinging bars, and teach a spaniel's tricks to the man-eating lion.

But the religious value, the formally religious value, of the circus is even more obvious than its moral value. For the circus, more than any other secular institution on the face of the earth, exemplifies—it may be said, flaunts—that virtue which is the very basis of religion, the virtue of faith.

Now, faith is the acceptance of truth without proof. The man who is told and believes that something contrary to his experience will happen has faith. And he who considers the psychology of the audience at a circus, he who (there are scientists sufficiently egotistic) looks into his own soul while a troupe of aërial acrobats are before his physical eyes, will see faith, strong and splendid.

It is not (as some pessimists who never went to a circus would have us believe) the expectation that the performer will fall and be dashed to pieces that makes people enjoy a dangerous act. People are like that only in the novels of D. H. Lawrence and the merry pastoral ballads of John Masefield. The circus audience gets its pleasure chiefly from its wholly illogical belief that the performer will not fall and be dashed to pieces; that is, from the exercise of faith. The audience enjoys its irrational faith that Mme. Dupin will safely accomplish the irrational feat of hanging by her teeth from a wire and supporting the weight of all the gold and pink persons who theoretically constitute her family. They enjoy the exercise of this faith, and they enjoy its justification. They really believe, just because a particularly incredible-looking poster tells them so, that there are in the side-show a man with three legs, a woman nine feet tall, and a sword swallower. They give up their money gladly, not to find that the poster was wrong, but because they have faith that it is right. There are no rationalists at the circus.

The audience has faith, and the performers—where would they be without it?—in small fragments, red and white on the tanbark floor. "If the sun and moon should doubt," remarked William Blake, "they'd immediately go out." If the lady who rides the motor cycle around the interior of the hollow brass ball, or the gentleman who balances a pool table, two lighted lamps and a feather on his left ear should doubt, they would go out just as promptly. The Peerless Equestrienne believes that she will land on her feet on the cantering white horse's broad rosined back after that double cartwheel. By faith the walls of Jericho fell down. By faith the Eight Algerian Aërial Equilibrists stayed up.

You may, of course, try this on your son. As he absorbs the strawed grape juice (degenerate substitute for the pink lemonade of antiquity!), munches the sibilant popcorn and the peanuts which the elephants declined, you may pour into his ears this disquisition on the religiosity of the greatest show on earth. In fact, the best time to preach to a child is while he is staring, with eyes as round as the balloons he is soon to acquire, at the splendors of the three rings. For then there is not the slightest chance of his answering you back, or hearing you.

They are modern enough for anyone, these wandering players. The gymnasts are at home on motor cycles, the clowns sport with burlesque aëroplanes. Yet they are wholesomely reactionary in other respects than those of having chariot races and such unaging feats of skill and strength as may have cheered the hearts of Cæsar's legionaries. They are reactionary in that they turn man's newest triumphs into toys. The motor cycle loses its dignity and is no longer an imposing proof of the truth of materialistic philosophy when a girl, built, it seems, of Dresden china, rides it on one wheel over hurdles and through a hoop of flame. And see! Yorick himself, with his old painted grin and suit of motley, makes a Blériot the butt of infinite jest.

The circus is vulgar. Its enemies say so; its friends, with grateful hearts assent. It is *vulgar,* of the crowd. To no play upon the stage can this lofty praise be given. For the circus as it is to-day would thrill and amuse and delight not only the crowd that to-day see it, but the crowd that might come from the days before the Flood, or from the days of our great-grandchildren's children. When Adam watched with pleased astonishment an agile monkey leap among the branches of an Eden tree, and laughed at the foolish face of a giraffe, he saw a circus. Delightedly now would he sit upon a rickety chair beneath a canvas roof, smell the romantic aroma of elephant and trampled grass, and look at wonders.

So it is that the vulgarity of the appeal of the circus—its democracy, if you prefer—has no temporal or geographic limits. And the performers themselves are a democracy—the acrobat who somersaults before death's eyes, the accomplished horseman, the amazing contortionist, the graceful juggler—all these are made equal by the ring, and, furthermore, they must compete for the applause of the throng with roller-skating bears, trained seals, and chalk-faced clowns. Yet there is aristocracy of the ring, and the subordination that Dr. Johnson praised. For here struts the ringmaster, with cracking whip, imperious voice, and marvelous evening clothes; the pageant with which the great show opened had its crowned queen; and even every troop of performing beasts has its four-footed leader.

The stage's glories have been sung by many a poet. But the circus has had no laureate; it has had to content itself with the passionate prose of its press agent. The loss is poetry's, not the circus's. For the circus is itself a poem and a poet—a poem in that it is a lovely and enduring expression of the soul of man, his mirth, and his romance, and a poet in that it is a maker, a creator of splendid fancies in the minds of those who see it.

And there are poets in the circus. They are not, perhaps, the men and women who make their living by their skill and daring, risking their lives to entertain the world. These are not poets; they are artists whose methods are purely objective. No, the subjective artists, the poets, are to be found in the basement, if the show is at the Garden, or, if the show be outside New York they are to be found in the little tents—the side-shows. This is not a mere sneer at the craft of poetry, a mere statement that poets are freaks. Poets are not freaks. But freaks are poets.

Rossetti said it. "Of thine own tears," he wrote, "thy song must tears beget. O singer, magic mirror hast thou none, save thine own manifest heart." Behold, therefore, the man on whom a crushing misfortune has come. He puts his grief into fair words, and shows it to the public. Thereby he gets money and fame. Behold, therefore, a man whom misfortune touched before his birth, and dwarfed him, made him a ridiculous image of humanity. He shows his misfortune to the public and gets money and fame thereby. This man exhibits his lack of faith in a sonnet-sequence; that man exhibits his lack of bones in a tent. This poet shows a soul scarred by the cruel whips of injustice; this man a back scarred by the tattooer's needles.

But the freaks would not like to change places with the poets. The freaks get large salaries (they seem large to poets), and they are carefully tended, for they are delicate. See, here is a man who lives although his back is broken. There is a crowd around him; how interested they are! Would they be as interested in a poet who lived although his heart was broken? Probably not. But then, there are not many freaks.

II

When Tom Gradgrind (who had, you remember, robbed the Coketown Bank, and been saved from punishment by the amiable intervention of Sleary's Circus) was living out his exile somewhere in South America, he often longed, Charles Dickens tells us in the engaging tale called "Hard Times," to be back in England with his sister. But what phase of his dismal boyhood and wasted later years did he see in his homesick dreams? What episodes of his life in England did it give him pleasure to relive in memory?

Dickens does not tell us. But no one who has read "Hard Times" and seen a circus needs to be told. The repentant exile, toiling under the tropic sun, had no affectionate recollections of Stone Lodge, his father's dreary mansion in Coketown, with its metallurgical cabinet, its conchological cabinet, and its mineralogical cabinet. Nor was it with anything approaching happiness that he thought of the Coketown Bank, the scene of some years of dull labor and of one moment of moral catastrophe.

He remembered, we may be sure, two things. He remembered appearing, with blackened face, an immense waistcoat, knee breeches, buckled shoes, and a mad cocked hat, as one of the comic servants of Jack the Giant-Killer at a certain Grand Morning Performance of Sleary's Circus. At the time he had been a fugitive from justice, but not even his fear and shame could keep his heart from stirring as he smelled the exhilarating odor of tanbark, trampled grass, and horses, heard the blare of the band, saw the glaring lights and the encircling tiers of applauding people, and knew that he—he, Tom Gradgrind, the oppressed, the crushed, the scientifically educated—was really and truly a circus performer!

And the other recollections, which, after the lapse

of many years, still made his heart beat more quickly, had to do with a gap in the pavilion in which Sleary's Circus once held forth in a suburb of Coketown—a gap through which young Tom Gradgrind delightedly beheld the "graceful equestrian Tyrolean flower-act" of Miss Josephine Sleary, and strained his astonished young eyes to watch Signore Jupe (none other than Sissy's father) "elucidate the diverting accomplishments of his highly trained performing dog Merrylegs."

And the reason why Sleary's Circus played so glorious a part in the memory of this broken exile was that it had brought into his most prosaic life all the poetry that he had ever known. Surrounded with facts, crammed with facts, educated and governed according to a mechanical system which was an extraordinary foreshadowing of our modern "efficiency," he was allowed two visits to an enchanted realm, two draughts of the wine of wizardry. Twice in his life he was mysteriously in communion with poetry.

There has been much talk recently about a renascence of poetry, and people have become excited over the fact that so many thousands of copies of Edgar Lee Masters' book have been sold, and so many more thousands of copies of the late Rupert

Brooke's Collected Poems. This is all very pleasant, but it doesn't mean that there has been a rebirth of poetry. Poetry cannot be reborn, for poetry has never died.

The circus draws us by the thousands to watch "desperately dangerous displays of unrivaled aërialism," and "the acme of expert equitation and acrobatic horsemanship" beneath the Diana-guarded roof of Madison Square Garden; even so it drew our fathers and their fathers before them to rickety wooden benches propped against great swaying canvas walls, in the days when Robinson and Lake displayed the wonders of the world in glorious rivalry with Hemings, Cooper and Whitby. Even so will the circus flourish in the days to come, when aëroplanes are cheaper than motor cars, and the war that began in August, 1914, is but a thing of dates and names in dusty textbooks. For poetry is immortal. And the circus is poetry.

What is the function of poetry? Is it not to blend the real and the ideal, to touch the commonplace with lovely dyes of fancy, to tell us (according to Edwin Arlington Robinson), through a more or less emotional reaction, something that cannot be said? And is not this exactly what the circus does? Most of its charm is due to the fact that all its wonders are in some way connected with our ordinary life. The elephant in his enclosure at the Zoölogical Gardens is merely a marvel; when he dances the tango or plays the cornet he allies himself with our experience, takes on a whimsical humanity, and thus becomes more marvelous. The elephant in the Zoo is an exhibit; the elephant tangoing in the tanbark ring is poetry.

And there is Zipp, the What-is-it? most venerable of freaks, whose browless tufted head and amazing figure have entertained his visitors since Phineas Taylor Barnum engaged him to ornament his museum on Ann Street. For all I know, Zipp is a poet—his smile is lyrical, and in his roving eyes there is a suggestion of vers libre. But at any rate, Zipp is a poem—a particularly charming poem when, in the procession of freaks which opens the performance, he gallantly leads round the arena that fantastically microcephalous young woman known to fame as the Aztec Queen. The Bearded Lady and the Snake Charmer and the Sword Swallower are poems—poems in the later manner of Thomas Hardy. And that delightfully diminutive chocolate-colored person who rejoices in the name of the Princess Wee-Wee—with her, in her dainty little golden-spangled gown, what lyric of Walter Savage Landor can compare?

It is the splendor of incongruity that gives the equestrian and aërial feats of the arena their charm, that incongruity which is the soul of romance. The creatures we see are the creatures we know, but they have most poetically changed places. It would be the mere prose of our daily life for birds to fly about close to the tent's roof, and for men and women to ring bells and sit in rocking chairs. It is the poetry of the circus that men and women fly about close to the tent's roof, and birds ring bells and sit in rocking chairs.

No one can describe a circus in prose. The industrious press agent of the circus long ago gave up the attempt, and resorted to impressionistic free verse, characterized by an ecstasy of alliteration. No one can adequately describe the involved contortions, swings, and dashes of a "family" of silk-clad adventurers on the flying trapeze. No faithful narrative of the grotesque buffetings of the chalk-faced clowns is in itself amusing—and yet the antics of these agile mimes have always been, will always be, irresistibly mirth-compelling. The magic of the circus is compounded of so many things—movement, sound, light, color, odor—that it can never be put into words. It is absurd to attempt to reflect it in prose, and it cannot be reflected in poetry because it is itself poetry; it is the greatest poem in the world.

And just as Sleary's Circus was the cup of poetry which benevolent fate held twice to the parched lips of young Thomas Gradgrind's soul, so is the circus of our day, with its regiment of clowns, its roller-skating bears and dancing elephants, its radiant men and women who pirouette on horseback and dart above our heads like swallows, a most wholesome and invigorating tonic for a weary and prosaic generation. We who every morning at the breakfast table read of war and desolation need to cheer our hearts with the burlesque battles of the clowns; we who ride in the subway need to exult when the charioteer, with streaming toga, guides his six white horses on their thunderous course; we whose eyes are daily on our ledgers and sales records need to lift them, if not to the stars, at least to the perilous wire on which a graceful pedestrian gayly flirts with death. We whose lives are prose may well be grateful for the circus, our annual draught of poetry; for the circus, the perennial, irresistible, incomparable, inevitable Renascence of Wonder.

THE ABOLITION OF POETS

EVER since certain vivacious Frenchmen put on funny little red nightcaps and remarked "Ça ira!" the inevitability of a reform has been the chief article of its propaganda. The Socialist orator says: "Socialism is coming upon us with the speed of the whirlwind and the sureness of the dawn." Therefore he mounts a soap-box and passionately urges six small boys, the town drunkard and a policeman to accelerate the whirlwind and encourage the dawn in its commendable habit of punctuality. The suffragist tells us: "The Votes for Women movement, like a mighty ocean, will break down the barriers of prejudice and flood the country." Therefore, like a perverted Mrs. Partington, she runs out with her little broom to help the ocean along. And so, humbly following these illustrious precedents, I advocate the abolition of poets because poets are rapidly abolishing themselves.

For one thing, they have given up the uniform. In the old days it was easy to recognize them.

THE ABOLITION OF POETS

They wore velvet jackets and sombreros, they let their hair hang over their shoulders, they were also, I believe, picturesquely ragged. When you saw M. Paul Verlaine in his great cloak, drinking absinthe at a table on the boulevard, you recognized him as a poet. But when you see Mr. Clinton Scollard in his decorous cutaway drinking a milk shake in a drug store, how are you to guess his profession?

Of course, there are people who look like poets. When your literary inclined maiden aunt from West Swansey, New Hampshire (by a sacred convention all maiden aunts are literarily inclined), visits New York, you take her to a restaurant which is supposed to be bohemian because it is near Washington Square. The macaroni is buoyantly elastic, the lettuce is wilted, the chicken tough, the wine a blend of acetic acid and aniline. But your aunt enjoys it, and she is vastly interested in the company.

She hunts for poets. "There!" she exclaims. "There is a poet! What is his name?" And she points to a romantic-looking youth with great mop of hair, a soft-collared flannel shirt, and a large black necktie.

You answer, wildly striving to keep your reputation for omniscience: "That? Why, that's Alfred

Noyes." Or "That's James Whitcomb Riley."
Or "That's Henry van Dyke." Your aunt is pleasantly thrilled, and she will entertain all West Swansey with the tale of this literary adventure. And
you drown your lie in a beaker of acid claret.

As a matter of fact, who is this big-necktied,
long-haired person? Perhaps he is a cabaret performer, and will presently give your aunt a novel
insight into the habits of the literati by rising to
sing with a lamentable air of gayety, "Funiculi,
Funicula." Perhaps he is one of those earnest
young men who have for their alma mater the dear
old Ferrer School. But in all probability he is
merely an innocent bystander who endeavors in
his dress to commemorate a visit to East Aurora.

The two great steps in the abolition of poets were
the shearing of Mr. Richard Le Gallienne and the
invention of East Aurora. When Mr. Le Gallienne's hair waved, a black and curly banner, before the literary legions of the world, then poets
lived up to their traditional reputation; courage-
ously they were picturesque. But when the fell
scissors did their brutal work, then poets donned
the garb of burgesses.

And then the more adventurous burgesses began
to dress like poets. Mr. Hubbard began the manu-

facture of large black neckties, and the Village Atheists all over America put them on. Everyone who had queer ideas about religion, economics, ethics or politics wore the necktie that had previously confined only lyric throats. Now when you see a man wearing two yards of black crêpe in front of his collar, do not expect him to sing you a madrigal. It is probable that his decoration signifies merely that he is opposed to vaccination.

And when the poets took to wearing prosaic clothes, they took also to following prosaic occupations. Is there now living a man who does nothing but write verse? I doubt that the most thorough explorer of contemporary letters could discover such an anachronism. Poets still write poetry, but the ancient art is no longer their chief excuse for existence. They come before the public in other and more commonplace guises.

Mr. T. A. Daly was until recently business manager of a weekly paper. Messrs. Bliss Carman, Richard Le Gallienne, Ford Madox Hueffer, Nicholas Vachell Lindsay, and eight thousand other poets write literary criticisms. Dr. Henry van Dyke preaches and is a diplomat. Mr. Rudyard Kipling preaches and is not a diplomat. All the poets have regular jobs. In the good old days it was different. Then Dr. Henry van Dyke, Mr. Tom Daly, and the rest of them would have done nothing all day and all night but write poetry and read it to each other as they sat and drank anisette or some other sweet, sticky cordial in a club named the Camembert Cheese, or something of the sort. They would have scorned editing anything less precious than The Germ or The Yellow Book. And as to writing book reviews—as well ask them to get married!

For a time Mr. Alfred Noyes kept the spirit of craft-integrity. He alone, among book reviewing, story writing, magazine editing versifiers, was solely a poet. But now even he has taken up a side line. First he delivered the Lowell lectures; then he became a university professor. Over his laurel wreath he has put a mortar-board.

But the departure of the poets from a strictly professional attitude toward life is only one side of the shield. The poets have become citizens; that is bad enough. But also the citizens have become poets. They do not call themselves poets, they merely write verse as casually as they write letters.

For one thing, the rhymed advertisement is more common now than ever before. Formerly, when the proprietor or advertising manager of a manufactory of automobiles or chewing gum or some other necessity of American life desired to celebrate his wares in verse, he went to some trouble and expense. He called in an impecunious literary man, that is, a literary man, and with some trepidation made what business men quaintly call a proposition. The poet considered the matter carefully, arranged the terms of payment, and insisted upon the exclusion of his name from the published composition, was supplied with material descriptive of his subject, and departed to his conventional garret. In the course of time he brought back the desired verses, was paid, and treated with mingled curiosity and awe by the men of affairs who had made use of his talents.

Now all is changed. The advertising managers started scabbing on the unorganized and individualistic poets and actually drove them off the job. Now, when a cough drop is to be made the subject of a sonnet-sequence what happens? Does a regular professional poet get a dollar a line for the work? He does not. The advertising manager sends the office boy out for a rhyming dictionary and writes the verses himself. Or else he lets the office boy write them.

But this is only one manifestation of this lamentable state of affairs. Another is the fact that most people are the authors of books of verse. People do not buy poetry, they do not read poetry, but they write it with amazing enthusiasm and industry. There are now at least four prosperous publishers who do nothing but bring out books at the expense of the authors, and their lists contain practically nothing but volumes of verse. The country clergyman, lawyer, or school teacher who has not written a volume of verse and paid from $100 to $500 to have it printed (with his portrait as frontispiece) is a rare bird indeed. These people never buy books of verse, and, of course, almost no copies of their own books are sold. But the fact remains that nearly everybody who can read and write makes verse, carelessly, casually, without effort or emotion. The shoemaker who wishes to call the attention of the public to his new stock of canvas shoes with green leather inserts lisps in numbers and the numbers come. And the man who has nothing to advertise but his own personality seizes authoritatively upon the Muse's hair and pulls it until she shrieks his praise.

It will be objected that what these people write is merely verse, not poetry; that no one considers them poets and that they do not claim the title.

THE ABOLITION OF POETS

But this is not a valid objection, it is thoroughly in accordance with my thesis. They write verse, and they are not poets; therefore they—all people, that is—believe that one need not be a professional poet to write verse any more than one need be a professional dishwasher to wash dishes. So poetry, as a distinct craft, utterly disappears; it does not even continue as a separate and special branch of unskilled labor.

Of course, there still exist people who take the making of verse somewhat seriously. But the loudest of them, those who most earnestly insist upon the importance of themselves and their art, are those ridiculous young people who call themselves Imagistes and Vorticists and similar queer names. And they deliberately take from poetry its characteristics of rhyme and rhythm and apply the name poetry to little chunks of maudlin prose. So they, too, are working for the abolition of poets and poetry.

There is an exquisite Socialist doctrine called "progressive poverty" or something of the sort, according to which we are to let conditions get worse and worse so that they may ultimately become unbearable. Then, it is said, the coöperative commonwealth will almost automatically come into being.

Perhaps this suggests a solution for the problem now under consideration. Let the few remaining professional poets resolutely abstain from writing verse; let verse be made only by patent medicine manufacturers and grocers and Imagistes and, in general, people totally ignorant of poetry. They will produce it in abundance; they will probably perfect some mechanical device, a poem-jenny, perhaps, which will produce a standard poem in a short time and gradually do away with the home-manufactured article.

In the course of time the patents on this device will be taken over by the Standard Oil Company, and poems of uniform perfection will be furnished at small cost to every house or apartment. Then, after some twenty-five years, there will come a reaction, a sort of craftsman, back-to-nature movement. Some adventurous person will make up a real poem of his own, and his friends will say, "How quaint! That is the way they did in the old days before the poem-jenny was invented. I rather like this poem. It has strength, simplicity, a primitive quality that I cannot find in the poems the Standard Oil Company sends up every week. Go on, Rollo, and see if you can make another one."

Thus encouraged, Rollo will make another poem,

and another, and rather histrionically will assume the picturesque old title of poet. Other poets will arise, and the Standard Oil Company will turn its attention to perfecting devices for the construction of novels. Poems made by hand by specialists will then be the only articles of the sort produced. In this way only can there ever be a genuine renascence of the ancient and honorable craft of poetry.

NOON-HOUR ADVENTURING

SUN worship, according to the latest religious census, is no longer a popular cult. This is a pity, for it was more respectable and more diverting than most of the forms of paganism that have superseded it.

But the sun is a good-humored deity; he showered his gifts no more generously of old on Teheran, whose walls were resonant with his praise, than now on faithless New York. Daily from his meridian he stretches forth his shining scimitar and strikes the fetters from the feet of young men, setting them free to walk the golden streets of an enchanted city.

The feet, I said, of young men. For men no longer young the noon hour is a time for the comfortable but unromantic occupation of eating. The man who usually takes a car to get from Thirty-third Street to Times Square, who occasionally lets the barber rub tonic on the top of his head, who carries blocks and dolls home on Saturday, who is morbidly interested in building loans and grass-seed, regards the noon hour as at worst a time for shopping and at best a time for eating. But to the young man, particularly to the young man for the first time a wage-earner in the city, the noon hour is a time for splendid adventuring.

It may be that there are young women for whom the luncheon hour is a gay thread of romance in the dull fabric of the working day. Of this I cannot speak with certainty; my observation indicates that they regard it merely as an opportunity to go, in chattering companies, to those melancholy retreats called tea rooms to amuse themselves with gossip and extraordinary ices. But the young man leaves his desk at the appointed hour as bravely as ever pirate vessel left its wharf, and sails forth to sparkling and uncharted seas.

Consider, for example, the case of James Jones. James spent his boyhood in a town less than a hundred miles from New York. Visits to the city were great events in his young life. He was taken there to buy clothing, to go to the theater, to visit unusually exciting relatives who lived in apartment houses, rode on elevators, and drew milk from dumb-waiters. During his collegiate career James made occasional trips to New York, always with the theater and the tavern as his objectives. Triumphantly now he feels himself actually a New York, a dweller in no mean city. Joyfully, therefore, he goes forth every noon to explore the territory of his new possession.

James is, let it be understood, nearer 20 than 25. He is beginning to regard his diploma with some disrespect, but he still wears his fraternity pin on an obscure corner of his waistcoat. Every Saturday morning he gets an envelope containing a $10 bill and a $5 bill, and he has already formulated in his mind an eloquent appeal which cannot fail, he believes, to increase that amount to $18.50. James endeavors to seem as sophisticated as the chauffeur of a taxicab; not for worlds would he betray the innocent delight with which he regards the city of his habitation.

With James's occupation from 9 in the morning until the luncheon hour we have no concern. Perhaps he sits on a high stool and ciphers in a great ledger, perhaps he haltingly dictates letters to a patronizing stenographer, perhaps he urges certain necessities or luxuries upon a suspicious public. The important fact of his life—for us and, in a measure, for him—is that once every day he answers the welcome summons of the unknown.

Luncheon is a tiresome obligation, quickly to be

fulfilled. His mother would be vexed to see him gulp his malted milk or bolt his sandwich. On some occasions, with a pleasant sense of recklessness, he enters a bar, and, with something of a flourish, consumes beer and free lunch. With some difficulty he refrains from looking over the swinging doors before leaving, as he did in his home town, to make sure that none of his neighbors are coming down the street.

James left his desk only six minutes ago and his luncheon is already over. There remain fifty-four precious minutes. Behold him tasting rapturously of every second of these minutes! Behind a cheap but decorative cigar he walks up, perhaps, Fifth Avenue, undeniably that excellent thoroughfare's possessor. For his delight is Diana poised on her tower of purple memories; the grass of Madison Square is greener than that of his father's lawn; tulips more vivid than these never bloomed in the rich gardens of Holland.

He is considered a sympathetic person, but at noon, I fear, his attitude is that of a realist. For he watches with ingenuous interest the antics of that drunkard on a park bench, and regards the arrival of the patrol wagon and summary removal of the culprit as a drama got up solely for his entertainment. Regrettable as it may seem, it is with heightened spirits that he continues his stroll.

Now he has reached a great bookshop which even the penniless find hospitable. "Some day," says James to himself, "two hundred copies of my novel will draw a crowd around this plate glass window." Mentally he arranges an effective window display and goes on to feast his eyes on vellum and sha-green, on calf delicately tooled and parchment gay with gold leaf and many colored inks. Sometimes he enters the shop (the clerks are indulgent to James and his kind) and, over the merry pages of *Jugend* and *La Vie Parisienne,* rejoices that his father made him study modern languages at college.

But literature must not claim too much of his fast-fleeting hour. There are shops at hand whose windows show things stranger than books; chairs and bedsteads eloquent of the genius of Adam and Heppelwhite; the massive silver platter on which old Wardle carved a Christmas goose when Mr. Pickwick was his guest; a mighty flagon that brimmed with red wine for Pantagruel; a carved jade bracelet from the brown arm of the Princess Badoura; the sword of Robert Bruce. All lands, all ages have sent their treasures to New York this noon for the entertainment of James Jones.

[74]

NOON-HOUR ADVENTURING

It may be that this square of Japanese embroidery, on which fantastic knights thrust tremendous javelins at red and green dragons under astonished willows, was made in Paterson, N. J. What of that? The colors are not therefore less bright. James is not a purchaser, he is merely a spectator of the greatest raree-show in the world. It is well for him to be deceived in the splendors displayed before him. Not so many years ago he would prefer a red glass ball to the Kohinoor and a hand organ with a monkey to a piano with Paderewski. James yet retains a receptivity almost infantile; but it would pain him to be told so.

They are not gregarious, at noon, these young discoverers of New York. They are selfish in their adventuring, for a vision shared is only half a vision. James, I know, is annoyed when he finds an acquaintance gobbling a sandwich at his luncheon counter or staring in a jeweler's window that he has come to regard as his own private property. On Sundays he is sociable enough; he is glad of a companion on his journeys across and up and down Manhattan, among the Italians and negroes of the upper west side, through the loud ghetto and speciously weird Chinatown, in the deliberate sylvanity of Central Park and the Bronx Gardens. In the

evening, too, he is not at all a recluse. But at noon
he has no appetite for conversation; he would not
have his attention taken from the strange streets
by an accustomed human being.

James has never ridden on a London bus, yet I
believe in the truth of his unspoken thought, that a
Fifth Avenue bus is the most excellent vehicle in
the world. The London bus depends for its charm
on a number of non-essential qualities; on the humor of its driver (are the chauffeurs of London's
electric buses also masters of epigram?), on the
quaintness and antiquity of the thoroughfare, on
the military efficiency of the traffic policemen, on
the philmayishness of the passengers. The Fifth
Avenue bus has one reason for existence: it shows
its passengers Fifth Avenue. No bus can do more.

So one may (if one is young enough to be so
foolish and so wise) ride, like the Gaikwar of Ba-
roda in his swaying howdah, high above the people
for a golden hour. He may start at uneasy Washington Square, where ancient respectability wars
with young bohemianism. Soon he looks down on
the throngs of new Americans that tramp the once
proud pavement. From his high seat he sees them,
the small, dark men and women who, like him, are
for a time released from labor. They move slowly

in great crowds, they eat frugal meals, the wares of curb-side peddlers, they talk and gesture incessantly. What does James think of them? I do not believe that his opinion is worth knowing.

But he enjoys, I know, the tour through the traffic-filled intersection of Broadway and Twenty-third Street, and he is not old enough to notice with regret the gradual deterioration of the latter street. Freed from the close company of baser vehicles, how triumphantly the bus whirrs up the broad street past the square, among the splendid shops and clubs and churches—the true New Yorker, I think, names them in this order. But James must not give too much attention to the lovely Gothic lines of St. Thomas's, or the lovely Byzantine lines of that pink chiffon lady in the landau—the luncheon hour draws to a close, and punctuality, he still believes, is a business virtue.

The brevity of this recess is essential to it. If the time be indefinitely increased, if the young adventurer be allowed all the morning and all the afternoon for his wandering, then all the zest goes out of the adventure. There is that trusted veteran employee in the corner of the office. He receives fabulous sums on pay day and may go out to luncheon whenever he desires, with no time clerk to censor him. He knows New York less than does James. But does his curiosity urge him forth to long adventures? Over his stale morning's paper in the deserted office, seated before his familiar task, he eats his sordid and wife-made luncheon!

But the noon adventurer is not limited to Fifth Avenue. The antique shops of Fourth Avenue charm him with pewter and brass, they cheer his heart with sun dials from English rose gardens and crucifixes from convents of Dante's land and time. At Twenty-third Street stalls he reads bits of forgotten writings and breathes the pleasant scent of worn calfskin. Perhaps on the 15-cent rack he comes upon a prize. Here is a little book of English verse by a Japanese poet. What is this faded inscription? "To Mary McLane from Yone Noguchi." The adventurer buys it, as the late Mr. Morgan would buy a Nuremburg Bible, and salves his economical conscience by rolling his own cigarettes for a while.

There are great sights for him, now and then. People who seemed, not so long ago, as legendary as Cuchulain and Cinderella appear to him on these noon expeditions, most startlingly human and real. He sees Mr. Roosevelt leave the Charities Building to enter a waiting taxicab. He visits the bootblack and in the chair next to him sits **Mr. Bliss Carman**, crowned with the huge black hat that is the livery of Vagabondia. On Fourteenth Street a big black-haired man and a little spectacled woman stop to laugh at the fortune-telling paroquets. With a delicious thrill the adventurer recognizes **Mr. Ben Reitman** and **Miss Emma Goldman**.

Nor are his adventures confined to seeing. There is plenty of action, sometimes. Once, as he stared into the windows of an Oriental rug shop, he was aware of a thin, hunted-looking man who demanded his attention.

"I beg your pardon, Sir," said the hunted-looking man, "but can you tell me where I can find a parnbroker?"

I do not know why the hunted-looking man said "parnbroker," instead of "pawnbroker," but James always tells the story this way.

"No," said James, truthfully, "I can't."

"The reason I wanna know is," said the hunted-looking man very rapidly, "I gotta very fine stone here. I got into a little trouble in a hotel uptown; I gotta sell it right away very cheap."

And from a dirty pasteboard box he drew what seemed to be a large diamond ring.

Now was the thoroughly interested James aware

of yet another stranger who sought his attention, a prosperous-looking man, who smoked a fat cigar and flourished a silver-headed stick, who seemed trying to caution James against buying the diamond.

James had only 35 cents in his pocket, and was not a buyer, but a spectator of jewelry anyway. The hunted-looking man withdrew slowly. Then said the prosperous-looking man to James:

"Excuse me for buttin' in, old man, but I didn't want to see you stung. Sometimes these here fellers got real stones, sometimes they got fakes. Now I'm a professional jeweler and I got my microscope that I look at diamonds with in my pocket. Now, you call that guy back and tell him I'm a friend of yours and I'll examine that stone and tell you if it's any good."

The hunted-looking man gave rather too dramatic a start of surprise when called back by the suspicious but curious James.

"It's worth $500," he said, "but I'll sell it for $50. I got into a little trouble at a hotel uptown, and I gotta sell it cheap."

Professionally, elaborately, impressively, the prosperous-looking man screwed a glass into his eye and squinted at the stone. Then, taking James several yards away from the hunted-looking man, he said: "That's a genuine stone worth easy $500 if it's worth a cent. I know a place they'll give us $500 for it this afternoon on account of me being in the trade. Now, you keep him here while I go round the corner and get $25 from my bank and then we'll buy that stone together and make $225 apiece before two hours is gone. I'll be right back."

And the prosperous-looking man vanished.

Then—as might have been expected—the hunted-looking man offered James the diamond for $25. "You can put one over on that big guy," he said. "Slip me $25 and we beat it before he gets back. You can clean up $450 on it. I'm afraid of that big guy; I think he's gone after a cop."

Now, these two confidence men had worked hard with James. He should not have taken such delight in their discomfiture as he climbed the steps of a bus and bade them farewell.

When he met the hunted-looking man and the prosperous-looking man together on Broadway a few days later they cut him, and I do not blame them. But they gave him a real adventure, at any rate, an adventure not to be met by those who squander their noon hour sitting dully in sedate restaurants.

Then there was the adventure of the picture gallery. James went on one occasion to a futurist exhibition in a tiny room not far from Madison Square. Galleries are not crowded at noon, but from the room that James approached came sounds not to be accounted for even by the crazy canvases on its walls. Of course James went in, and found a futurist painter wrestling with the agent of a collection agency. The combatants rose, and demanded James's name and address, that he might. be summoned to court as a witness to assault and battery. But he never received either summons. Perhaps it was because he gave his name as Henry Smith of Yonkers.

Episodes like these have little charm for the middle-aged or for young men prematurely aged by spending their childhood in New York. These have their compensations, no doubt; their lives are not utterly bleak. But not for them is the daily romance of the young man who has just come to the city, who enjoys the proud novelty of working for wage, to whom every noon come sweet and strange the streets' compelling voices.

SIGNS AND SYMBOLS

THOSE people whom an hostile fate has made both athletes and reformers have among their aversions one which they proclaim with an enthusiasm so intense as to be almost infectious. They dislike passionately the harmless, unnecessary sign board when it has been so placed as to become a feature of the rural landscape. Wooden cows silhouetted against the sunset only irritate them by their gentle celebrations of malted milk; the friendliest invitation to enjoy a cigarette, a corset or a digestive tablet fills them with anger if it comes from the face of a sea-shadowing cliff or from among the ancient hemlocks of a lofty mountain.

There is, of course, a modicum of reason in their attitude. It is wrong to paint the lily at all; it is doubly wrong to paint "Wear Rainproof Socks" across its virgin petals. It is wrong to mar beauty; that is an axiom of all æsthetics and of all ethics. It would be wrong, for example (although it would be highly amusing), to throw by means of a magic lantern great colored phrases against Niagara's sheet of foam; it would be wrong to carve (as many earnest readers of our magazines believe has been done) an insurance company's advertisement on the Rock of Gibraltar.

But the æsthete-reformer, in condemning such monstrosities as these, condemns merely an hypothesis. And since the hypothesis obviously is condemnable, he starts a crusade against the innocent facts upon which the purely hypothetical evil is based. It is wrong to mar the snowy splendor of the Alps; therefore, he says, the Jersey meadows must not bear upon their damp bosom the jubilant banner of an effective safety-razor. The sylvan fastness of our continent must be saved from the vandal; therefore, he says, you may not advertise breakfast food on a hoarding in the suburbs of Paterson.

If the æsthete-reformers in question would examine the subject dispassionately they would see that there is really nothing in the sign board as it stands to-day about which they may justly complain. Advertisers do not deliberately annoy the public; they would not be so foolish as to seek to attract people by spoiling what was beautiful. It must be remembered that a landscape may be rustic and yet not beautiful.

SIGNS AND SYMBOLS

The æsthete does not dislike, instead he hails with enthusiasm, a worn stone bearing the dim inscription "18 Mil. To Ye Cittye of London." Why then should he shudder when he sees a bright placard which shouts "18 Miles to the White Way Shoe Bazaar, Paterson's Pride"? To my mind there is a vivacity and a humanness about the second announcement utterly lacking in the first. The æsthete dotes upon the swinging boards which with crude paintings announce the presence of British inns. If "The Purple Cow, by Geoffrey Pump. Entertainment for Man and Beast" delights his soul, why does he turn in angry sorrow from "Stop at the New Mammoth Hotel when you are in Omaha—500 Rooms and Baths—$1.50 up—All Fireproof"? It is a cheerful invitation, and it should bring to jaded travelers through the track-pierced wastes a comfortable sense of approaching welcome and companionship.

There are many things which might be said in favor of urban sign boards, especially in favor of those elaborate arrangements in colored lights which make advertisements of table waters and dress fabrics as alluringly lovely as the electrical splendor of the first act of Dukas' "Ariane et Barbe Bleu." But in the city the sign board is always something supererogatory; it may be decorative, but it is not necessary. One does not need a six-yard announcement of a beer's merit when there are three saloons across the street; even the placards of plays line almost uselessly the thoroughfares of a district in which the theaters are conspicuous.

But in the country the sign boards are no luxuries but stern necessities. This the æsthete-reformers fail to see because they lack a sense of the unfitness of things. It is their incongruity which gives to rustic sign boards the magic of romance. The deliberately commercial announcement, firmly set in an innocent meadow or among the eternal hills, has exactly the same charm as a buttercup in a city street or a gray wood-dove fluttering among the stern eaves of an apartment house.

What a benefaction to humanity these rural sign boards are! To the farmer they are (in addition to being a source of revenue) a piquant suggestion of the wise and wealthy city. He loves and fears the city, as mankind always loves and fears the unknown. Once he thought that it was paved with gold. He must have thought so, otherwise how could he have accounted for the existence of gold bricks? He is less credulous now, but still the big signs down where the track cuts across the old pasture pleasantly thrill his fancy.

And what would a railway journey be without these gay and civilizing reminders? They hide the shame of black and suicidal bogs with cheery hints of vaudeville beyond, they throw before the privacy of farmhouses a decent veil of cigarette advertisements. He who speeds vacation-ward from the city is glad of them, for they remind him that he is where factories and huge shops may come only in this pictured guise, thin painted ghosts of their noisy selves. He who gladly speeds back to domesticity and the ordered comforts of metropolitan life sees them as welcoming seneschals, glorious advance-posts of civilization. They are the least commercial of all commercial things, they are as human and as delightful as explorers or valentines.

THE GREAT NICKEL ADVENTURE

WHENEVER I read Mr. Chester Firkins' excellent poem "On a Subway Express" I am filled with amazement. It is not strange that Mr. Firkins turned the subway into poetry, it is strange that the subway does not turn every one of its passengers into a poet.

There are, it is true, more comfortable means of locomotion than the subway; there are conveyances less crowded, better ventilated, cooler in Summer, warmer in Winter. A little discomfort, however, is an appropriate accompaniment of adventure. And subway-riding is a splendid adventure, a radiant bit of romance set in the gray fabric of the work-a-day world.

The aëroplane has been celebrated so enthusiastically in the course of its brief life that it must by now be a most offensively conceited machine. Yet an aëroplane ride, however picturesque and dangerous, has about it far less of essential romance than a ride in the subway. He who sails through the sky directs, so nearly as is possible, his

[88]

course; he handles levers, steers, goes up or down, to the left or the right. Or if he is a passenger, he has, at any rate, full knowledge of what is going on around him, he sees his course before him, he can call out to the man at the helm: "Look out for that comet's hair! Turn to the left or the point of that star will puncture our sail!"

Now, unseen dangers are more thrilling than those seen; the aëroplane journey has about it inevitably something prosaic. This is the great charm of the subway, that the passengers, the guards, too, for that matter, give themselves up to adventure with a blind and beautiful recklessness. They leave the accustomed sunlight and plunge into subterranean caverns, into a region far more mysterious than the candid air, into a region which since mankind was young has been associated with death. Before an awed and admiring crowd, the circus acrobat is shut into a hollow ball and catapulted across the rings; with not even a sense of his own bravado, the subway passenger is shut into a box and shot twenty miles through the earth.

Once there lived on West One Hundred and Eighty-second Street a man of uncompromising practicality, a stern rationalist. He was as advanced as anything! He believed in the material-

istic interpretation of history, economic determin-
ism, and radium; this, he said, with some pride, was
his Creed. Often he expressed his loathing for
"flesh-food," more frequently for "Middle Class
morality," most frequently for faith. "Faith is
stupidity," he would say. "Look before you leap!
It makes me sick to see the way people have been
humbugged in all ages. The capitalist class has
told them something was true, something nobody
could understand, and they've blindly accepted it,
the idiots! I believe in what I see—I don't take
chances. I don't trust anybody but myself."

Yet every day this man would give himself up
to the subway with a sweet and child-like faith. As
he sat in the speeding car, he could not see his
way, he had no chance of directing it. He trusted
that the train would keep to its route, that it would
stop at Fourteenth Street and let him off. He
could not keep it from taking him under the river
,and hurling him out into some strange Brooklyn
desert. When he started for home in the evening,
he read the words "Dyckman Street" on the car
window with a medieval simplicity, and on the guar-
antee of these printed words, placed there by
minions of the capitalist class, he gave up the privilege of directing his course. The train, he believed,

would not at Ninety-sixth Street be switched off to a Bronx track; the sign told him that he was safe, and he believed it.

So the subway caused him to exercise the virtue of faith, made him, for a time, really a human being. Perhaps it is the sharing of this faith that makes a subway crowd so democratic. Surely there is some subtly powerful influence at work, changing men and women as soon as they take their seats, or straps.

For one thing, they become alike in appearance. The glare of the electric light unifies them, modifying swarthy faces and faces delicately rouged until they are nearly of one hue. Then, the differences of attitude are lost, and attitudes are great instruments of subordination. The ragged bootblack does not kneel at the broker's feet; he sits close beside him, or perhaps, comfortably at rest, watches the broker clutch a strap and struggle to keep his footing.

"Tired clerks, pale girls, street-cleaners, business men, boys, priests and sailors, drunkards, students, thieves"—all gain a new sincerity. Neither the millionaire's imperiousness nor the beggar's professional humility can make the train go faster, so both are laid aside. Distinctions of race and caste grow insignificant, as in a company confronting one peril or one God. This is not theory, it is fact. The subway passenger purchases a nickel's worth of speed and he must take with it a nickel's worth of democracy.

Perhaps it is the youthful romanticism of America which makes our subways so much more exciting than those of Europe. The Englishman is too cautious and too conservative to trust himself away from the earth's surface more than two minutes at a time. So the trains that run through the London tube are tame, cowardly things. They timidly run underground for half a mile or so and pop their heads out into the air and sunlight or fog at every station.

But the New York subway train is ready to take a chance. It dives into the earth and "stays under," like a brave diver, for an hour at a time. And when it does emerge, what splendor attends its coming! There is a glimmer of sunshine at the One Hundred and Sixteenth Street Station; the blue and white of the walls and pillars reflect a light not wholly artificial. Then there is a brief stretch of fantastically broken darkness. Passengers in the first car can see ahead of them, at Manhattan Street, a great door of sunshine. At last there is

a strange change in the rumble of the wheels, for
the echoing roof and walls are gone, and the train
leaves its tunnel not to run humbly over the ground,
but to rise higher and higher until it comes to a
sudden halt above the chimneys and tree tops. To
say that the grub becomes a butterfly does not fit
the case, for the grub is a slow-moving beast and
a butterfly's course is capricious. Rather, it is as
if, by some tremendous magic, a great snake became a soaring eagle.

And how keenly all the passengers enjoy their
few seconds in the open air! When they hurried
down the steps to the train, they were scornful of
the atmosphere they were leaving, they had no
thought of tasting wind and watching sunlight.
Now they are become, for the moment, connoisseurs
of these delectable things; they wish the train would
linger at Manhattan Street, not inevitably plunge
at once into its roaring cavern. But the train is
wise, it knows brevity is essential to all exquisite
things, so it gives its passengers only an evanescent
glimpse of the glories they have just now learned
to appreciate.

This is a part of the great conspiracy of the subway. It is regarded only as a swift and convenient
and uncomfortable carrier, and it has no wish to be

otherwise interpreted. But those who have studied it know the hidden purposes it constantly and effectively serves. It is showing our generation the value of mankind's commonest and most precious gifts, by taking them away.

Now, it is good for man or beast to stand on solid ground in the sunlight, breathing clean air. Also fellowship is good, and the talk of friends. We forgot the value of these, we shut ourselves up in dark rooms and we spared no time to social exercise. Then—to punish and cure our folly—came the subway, making our journeys things close and dark in which conversation is a matter of desperate effort. And now how kind and talkative are people who go home together from the subway station after their daily disciplinary ride! They are grateful, too—although it may be subconsciously—for the familiar sights and sounds of the earth, for houses and streets and light that does not come from a wire in a bottle. They take gladly the great common things; they are simple, natural, democratic.

So they spend much of their leisure out of doors, these men and women who are underground two hours every weekday. In the evenings and on Sunday afternoons, they walk the pleasant streets with eager delight. They are curious about the loveliness far beneath which they daily speed. They have learned something of the art of life.

Of course, the subway has its incidental charms —its gay fresco of advertisements, for instance, and its faint mysterious thunder when it runs near the surface of the street on which we stand. But its chief service to man—perhaps its reason for existence—is that it gives him adventure. In this adventure he meets the spirit of faith and the spirit of democracy, which is an aspect of charity. And by their influence he becomes, surely though but for a time, as a little child.

THE URBAN CHANTICLEER

IF the rooster selected tree-tops for his roosting, crowed mournfully at the moon, and were a wild, unfriendly bird, every man's hand would be against him. But we forgive him his ugliness and conceit, not only because he is a dutiful citizen of the barnyard, but also because now, as in the days of the noble Horatio, he obligingly acts as "trumpet to the morn." On account of this romantic and sometimes useful custom, he wears a sentimental halo. M. Rostand has made him the hero of a drama. When will some wise playwright celebrate his urban prototype, the alarm clock?

The spirit in which this question is asked is not wholly one of mockery. For the alarm clock is close to humanity; in the city household, few bits of furniture are more personal and necessary. It is a faithful servant, this loud-voiced creature of steel and glass, obedient, punctual, patient. And its association with its owner, I had almost written its master, is so peculiarly intimate as to give it a personality and an attitude toward life.

THE URBAN CHANTICLEER

In the first place, it is irresistibly egotistic. There are some usual possessions which become subconscious things, their identities merging with the shadows of the vague land of habit. One may, for instance, possess a watch and yet not be aware of the watch as he is aware of his alarm clock. He lifts it from and returns it to his pocket; he winds it, with a gesture almost involuntary; he takes his information from his dial as thoughtlessly as he takes his breath from the atmosphere. Though it be made of fine gold, cunningly chased and blazoned with precious stones, it is to him, after the first delight of its acquisition, the unregarded means to an important end. So long as it serves him unprotestingly, he thinks of it no more than of his soul. People do not specifically ask him to consult his watch, they ask, "What time is it?" and even "Have you the time?"

Not thus does an alarm clock sink into oblivion. At least twice in twenty-four hours its owner must be vividly aware of its existence. It imperiously demands of him conscious action. In the morning clangorously, at night dumbly, it insists on attention. He must with thought adjust its mechanism, he must give it intelligent orders. And whether he rises at its summons or instead shuts out with a pillow its voice and that of conscience, he cannot ignore it. By no effort of will could Frankenstein forget his monster.

Not that the alarm clock is always a thing monstrous and threatening. It obeys orders with soldierly exactness but its sympathy is most unmartial. Routine cannot deaden its sensitivity. True, its ordinary note is something dry and monotonous. This comes from its perfect sense of the fitness of things; the call to business should be business-like. But what triumphant peals burst from its tiny belfry when it bids you rise and put on robes of honor! It can mimic the proud mirth of wedding bells; it knows the mighty song that rang from all the towers of London to cheer Dick Whittington. And that it can utter harsh and strident grief, those know who lie down with Sorrow and must awaken with her.

Even the most materialistic man has for his alarm clock a shame-faced personal regard. He speaks of it deprecatingly, with a humorous show of indignation. He tells how he maltreated it, knocked it from the mantel, smothered it with blankets, and there is a note of almost paternal exultation in his voice when he describes its persistence in ringing.

Franker souls actually parade what may be

termed their alarm-clockophilia. A friend of mine, one Carolus Dillingham, talks by the hour of his Nellie. Nellie is not, to the casual observer, an alarm clock of extraordinary merit. She was constructed many years ago and her nickel-plating is nearly gone. She is a small, weak-looking thing, with a great dome absolutely out of proportion to her rickety body. A result of her ridiculous construction is that when the alarm rings, she becomes slightly overbalanced, trembles, and moves a fraction of an inch forward on her feeble legs.

This, according to Carolus, is her chief charm. "I put Nellie," he says, "on the very edge of the shelf by the foot of my bed. When she rings in the morning she topples off and lands on the blankets. So I don't need to get up and walk across the cold floor. I can just reach out and choke her. I think she is the most faithful alarm clock in the world."

One little regarded virtue of the alarm clock is its sturdy democracy. It belongs irrevocably to the people, nothing can make it a snob. There is a watch for every rank; there are coarse peasant watches, fat bourgeois watches, and watches delicately aristocratic. But the alarm clock in the tenement of the laborer is the exact duplicate of that which wakens his employer; an alarm clock's an alarm clock for a' that. America will never really be a decadent nation until its alarm clocks are jeweled and soft-voiced.

The captious critic may object that the reason for the plainness of alarm clocks is that their use is restricted to what is loosely called "the working class." There is some truth in this.

Up to the present I have never witnessed the awaking of an aristocrat, or even of a captain of industry, but I suppose that they are hailed in soft tones by liveried menials, who bring them golden trays absolutely overflowing with breakfast food and remarkably thick cream. But aristocrats and captains of industry are rare birds, and all other people must have alarm clocks.

All other people, that is, who live in cities. For the alarm clock, in spite of its numerous excellences, is as inappropriate in the country as rouge on a milkmaid. The farmer must try to live up to his craft, and one of the æsthetic duties is to depend on mechanism as little as possible. His wife should rise when she hears the poultry saluting the dawn. Then, so nearly as I remember her obligations, she should go out on the front porch and blow a conchshell until her husband wakes up.

THE URBAN CHANTICLEER

The dweller in the suburbs is a creature of compromise. He grows vegetables and keeps chickens, perhaps he grows vegetables for the use of the chickens, and he cultivates a rural manner of speech. But he spends most of his waking hours in the city and every night he brings out with him on the five-twenty-seven some device to alter the simplicity of the country. He is an ambiguous creature, analogous to the merman. And the conspicuous symbol of his ambiguity is his alarm clock. It is in ruralia but not of it. It stands by a window that opens on an orchard, but it indicates the factory and market-place. It is a link between its owner's two personalities, it is the skeleton at the feast, reminding him, when he comes in from weeding the strawberry patch, that he must get up at a quarter to seven the next morning and hurry to the noisy train. Never does an alarm clock look so blatantly mechanical as when it stands in a cottage of one of the people barbarously termed "commuters."

For in the city, where everything is mechanical, the alarm clock seems pleasantly personal. It is at home there, it is perfectly in keeping with its surroundings. It takes on as comfortable an air of domesticity as the most ornate Swiss timepiece that ever said "Cuckoo"; it is contented, sociable, a member of the family. There is a sense of strangeness in the apartment that has no alarm clock; it is like a catless fireside.

And by association with the other sounds of awaking life, which even in the most sordid slum have about them something of energy and hope, the morning chorus of alarm clocks, echoing down the paved canyons from six to eight, make, in the ears of the unprejudiced listener, a cheerful noise. With them comes the mysterious creaking of the dumb-waiter as it ascends with the milk, an adequate substitute for the lowing of the herd. Kitchens and kitchenettes take on new life, and issue grateful odors of coffee and bacon. And babies, seeing that their weary parents are leaving them, decide at last that it is time to go to sleep.

An alarm clock can, on occasion, preach a sermon that would arouse the envy of Savonarola. When the jaded reveler returns to his home at daybreak, wastes ten minutes in a frantic attempt to awaken the elevator boy, and climbs, with cursing and gnashing of teeth, the eight flights of stairs that lead to his apartment, then nothing more sharply reminds him of his truancy than the voices of the alarm clocks calling to each other in the bedrooms of his virtuous neighbors.

Not even the laziest or the weariest man can hate the alarm clock as he does the factory whistle. The shrill blast that comes every morning from the iron throat of this monster has in it a note of contemptuous menace. The tired laborers awaken at their master's bidding; there is something unnatural about this abrupt wholesale termination of sleep. But the discipline of the alarm clock is another matter; he who hears it listens, it may be said, to his own voice. He himself has set it, he has fixed the very moment of his own awaking. And there is dignity in observing rules self-imposed, however irksome they may be. The alarm clock is the symbol of civilization, that is, of voluntary submission, of free will obedience.

The careful reader will be aware that many aspects of this excellent device have been neglected in this brief consideration. I have said nothing of the alarm clock's sense of humor and of its willingness to become a party to practical jokes. I have said nothing of how it may be pleased, of its pride, for instance, in being referred to as an "alarum clock." But it has one characteristic which I must mention, its usefulness to the suddenly rich.

There is a delightful sort of novel, Mrs. Frances Hodgson Burnett wrote one, and so did Mr. H. G. Wells, which deals with the adventures of a young man who has unexpectedly inherited a fortune. Samuel Warren's "Ten Thousand a Year" is perhaps the greatest example of this manner of fiction. Well, if I were T. Tembarom, or Kipps, or Tittlebat Titmouse (Dr. Warren's hero), my alarm clock would be necessary for my first act of celebration. Perhaps I should throw it from a window, perhaps I should remove its bell, perhaps I should merely enjoy letting it run down. At any rate, its presence would be necessary to the complete enjoyment of my new freedom.

DAILY TRAVELING

GIVE a dog a bad name and hang him. Call the custom of daily travel "commuting" and deliver it over to the whips of the scorner. The intransitive verb "to commute" is a barbarous thing; he who is called "commuter" is thereby rudely and ungrammatically taunted with journeying at reduced rates, with being (terrible thought!) the recipient of a railway's charity.

It is lamentable that so picturesque a habit as daily railway travel should be thus misnamed. That it is a picturesque habit is perceived by anyone who takes the trouble to consider it scientifically, shutting resolutely from his mind the odium brought upon it by its odious name. Suppose, for instance, that you were to go into the tap-room of the Mermaid Tavern some winter evening during the reign of the, so to speak, Good Queen Bess. The venerable Mr. Alfred Noyes would lead you to the table always reserved for Messrs. Shakespeare, Marlowe and Jonson. You would take from your pocket your commutation ticket, and, holding aloft that cabalistically inscribed oblong of colored cardboard, would sonorously declaim:

"By means of this talisman I daily fly across leagues of the New World, from my cottage in a primeval forest to the heart of a mighty city. It enables me to lead two lives; I am on week days urban, sophisticated, a man of commerce; at night and on Sundays I am a smocked yokel, innocent among my innocent vegetables. This little square of cardboard enables me to ride in a splendid vehicle propelled by Nature herself more swiftly than the wind, a vehicle which laughs at time and obliterates space. The masters of romance, bowing in homage, have bestowed upon me the mystic and awful name 'commuter.'"

Such a tale would draw Marlowe from his Malmsey and thrill the stout heart of mighty Ben. And Avon's bard, charmed by a fact more golden than all his imaginings, would augustly murmur "Very good, Eddie!"

It is a picturesque thing, this daily trip between the meadows and the pavements. By general consent, a vagabond is the most romantic of men; an allusion to the open road, wandering feet or the starlight on one's face is sufficient to turn an ordinary rhymer into that radiant being, a "tramp-poet." Then what glory must cling to those habitual vagabonds, those devotees of the steel highway, whom we call commuters. The common tramp seldom covers more than ten miles from sunrise to sundown; as a rule his pilgrimage is even briefer. Yet he is called a knight of the open road and even the staidest householder has a sneaking admiration for him. The gypsy is no true vagabond, for he takes with him his wife, children, dogs, furniture, and even his canvas-roofed house. Yet our writers, from Borrow to Kipling, delight to urge us to ha' done with the tents of Shem, dear lass, and follow the Romany patteran. The only authentic vagabond is he who every day goes thirty miles from his rural home to the city and every night thirty miles back, diving through mountains, plunging under rivers; twice on every week-day, a wanderer more free and venturesome than Lavengro himself.

But its picturesqueness is not the sole recommendation of daily railway travel. The greatest of its numerous virtues is that it is democratic, the only absolutely democratic institution in the United States of America. It is the mighty leveler, the irresistible enemy of social subordination.

In a city, town or village in which the citizens remain night and day there can be no true democracy. The intentions of its inhabitants may be excellent, but circumstances will be stronger. There is the minister, there is the banker, there is the doctor, there is the grocer, there is the cobbler, there is the minister's hired man. If a New England rural community is under observation there will also be noted the village atheist, the village drunkard, and the village Democrat. The population is sharply divided into classes; there may be friendliness among the various grades of humanity, there may be liberty, but there can be no fraternity, no equality.

How different is the community in which people merely dwell, having their business elsewhere! What is their occupation? They go to The City— that is sufficient answer to admit them to fellowship. If curiosity be still unsatisfied, there is the mention of the name of a great firm, and all is well.

The cobbler, you see, keeps his last in the city, away from his home and his neighbors; he does not stick to it, as the unpleasant adage bids him. As he sits on his red velvet chair, enjoying with his neighbors tobacco smoke, rapid travel, and the news of the world, who shall say whether he deals in shoes or in empires? Next to him is Dusenbury, who in addition to going to New York, goes to Wall Street, rumor has it. What does he do in Wall Street? Does he corner the wheat market or clean out waste baskets? Those who know, who say to him, "Sir" or "Hey, you," are not his companions on the 7.57.

There is a certain charm about what is called, ridiculously enough, a "commuting town," which is altogether lacking in other communities. A "commuting town" is wholly a place of homes— not of homes diluted with offices, factories and shops. It is therefore the quintessence of domesticity, being domestic with an intensity which no village which is remote from the centers of civilization, which furnishes employment and supplies to its own citizens can hope to approach.

Such a town is daily divided and joined, diminished and completed, thereby keeping in a state of healthy activity. The 7.57 takes away, the 5.24 brings back. These recurrent separations and reunions are not without their ethical and emotional value.

INCONGRUOUS NEW YORK

THAT dislike of the obvious which is the chief characteristic of American humor is clearly exemplified in the names of most of New York's streets.

The dwellers in a great European city would give their proudest avenue of great shops and rich clubs some dignified and significant title, like the Rue de la Paix or the Friedrichstrasse. The Asiatics would give it a name more definitely descriptive and laudatory, like "The Street of the Thousand and One Mirrors of Delight." The New Yorkers, "laconic and Olympian," designate it by a simple numeral. They call it Fifth Avenue.

It comes partly from the national reticence, this prosaic name of a poetic thoroughfare. It is a manifestation of that attitude of mind which makes us to call a venerated and beloved statesman merely "Old Abe," when the English would call him "the Grand Old Man" and the Italians "the Star-crowned Patriarch." Also it is a phase of our democracy. We will not seem to exalt one avenue over another by giving it a fairer name; Fifth Avenue sounds to the uninitiated no more wealthy and aristocratic than Fourth Avenue. Indeed, if there be any partiality in the awarding of names, it would seem to be exercised in favor of First Avenue or Avenue A.

It may be objected that the sponsors of Fifth Avenue did not foresee its destined splendor. But this fact does not alter the case; we continue to call it Fifth Avenue, whereas Europeans would alter its name to something more appropriate to its grandeur.

There was a pilgrim from the Five Towns who said that Fifth Avenue was architecturally the finest street in the world. This might pass for a guest's flattery, were it not that Mr. Arnold Bennett is of a nation which does not count gracious insincerity among its vices. New York must blushingly admit the truth of his judgment.

It is not (he said) harmonious. Its beauty is made up of units of beauty related only by position. This, too, is characteristically American. Each building must have its distinctive excellence.

To give a street of wonders an austere name, to build palaces and fill them with offices and shops—these are the acts by which Americans are known.

And especially does the New Yorker delight in the whimsical, the inconsistent, the unexpected. He is like a child who likes to dig in the sand with a silver spoon and to eat porridge with a toy shovel.

And this delicate perversity has its refreshing aspect. Fifth Avenue, surely, is a thing to admire in the new sense as well as the old. It sometimes suggests, perhaps, the ill-natured definition of a New Yorker as a man who, when he makes a set of chimes, puts it in a life insurance building. But it more often suggests a restatement of this definition; that is, that a New Yorker is a man who, when he makes a life insurance building, puts a set of chimes in it.

Now, certain masters of the mirthless science of psychology teach that humor depends on incongruity. Whether or not this is true, incongruity has much to do with making life worth while. For incongruity is the soul of romance.

Nobility, love, courage, beauty—the possession of these qualities does not give to a man or a woman romantic charm. A person is a hero or a heroine of romance because he or she lives in a contrasting place or age. For example, a cowboy riding a bucking bronco and whirling his lariat under a canvas roof in some sedate Eastern town is properly considered by the spectators to be a romantic figure. A cowboy engaged in the same interesting occupations on a Texas ranch would not be considered a romantic figure by his neighbors. It is incongruity of environment that romantically transforms him.

People and things of bygone ages are romantic to us because the years have gilded them. They were not romantic to their contemporaries. Says Edwin Arlington Robinson:

> Minniver loved the Medici
> And eyed a khaki suit with loathing;
> He missed the mediæval grace
> Of iron clothing.

Exactly. Minniver Cheevy was a true romanticist. A plumed knight, armed cap-a-pie, is a romantic figure when we merely see him through the years from our modern surroundings by means of imagination's powerful lens; he would be a figure even more romantic if we could actually see him shake his lance and lead his warriors against a drab-suited, machine-like company of present-day soldiers. Why, even horse cars, commonplace enough in their day, take on a certain sentimental luster when they lie abandoned in the outskirts of cities proud with electricity. And a subway train will one day be as romantic a spectacle as a stage coach.

Sometimes a building is deliberately given the romance of incongruity. This certainly is the case with the New York Stock Exchange. This splendid Grecian temple, with its lofty columns and noble façade, would, if it stood in ancient Athens, be, of course, beautiful, but in no respect romantic. It is romantic because it is in a place where it would not naturally be expected and because it is devoted to uses for which it does not seem to have been intended. If the god therein worshiped were not Mammon, but altisonant Jupiter, if white-robed priests found the future prefigured in the warm blood of the lambs therein sacrificed—then the building which now houses the clamoring merchants would be merely dignified and practical and not, as it is today, romantic.

The use of this Grecian temple as a counting house is a splendid example of the poetic tendency of a popular mind. The common business terms— "Bull" and "Bear," for example—are incongruous, and therefore romantic. And a successful business man is not realistically called a successful business man; he is romantically called a "merchant prince" or a "captain of industry."

But most of New York's romantic places get their glory not by plan, but by the accident of design. You turn the corner from a sombre street lined by tall concrete and steel structures that obviously are of your own period and come suddenly upon a mellow bit of New Amsterdam. You would not be surprised to see old Peter Stuyvesant stump down Coenties Slip and drop in for his morning's Hollands at "22½," across the way. There are streets and squares and alleys in downtown New York that look now exactly as they did when Times Square was a cow pasture and the Bowery really bowery. But these places were not romantic to the citizens of that time; they would not be romantic to us if by some strange backward transmigration of souls we should inhabit a vanished century.

No, we are fortunate to live when Battery Place and Coenties Slip have acquired romance's glamour. Incongruity is the soul of romance. And these quaint time-hallowed places have the loveliest sort of incongruity—the magical incongruity of archaisms.

IN MEMORIAM: JOHN BUNNY

THERE was a clown named Joseph Grimaldi. And when his agile limbs and mobile features were stilled by death there lingered in the minds of the thousands who had laughed at him in Sadler's Wells and Covent Garden only the memory of their mirth.

There was a clown named John Bunny. Now he is dead. But we still may see, and our children's children may see, the gestures and grimaces that made him a welcome visitor in every quarter of the globe. For by grace of the motion-picture camera, John Bunny's art endures.

It is art, this power of conveying ideas without the use of words, of exciting laughter by actually being, instead of saying, a joke. It is the difficult and venerable art of the clown, the art of the shaven-headed mime in variegated robes whose antics drove care from Cæsar's furrowed brow, the art of Garrick's harlequin friend, John Rich, and of the mirth-compelling Pinkethman, whose "frolic gestures" won the praise of Alexander Pope.

IN MEMORIAM: JOHN BUNNY

Of course, John Bunny could play in speaking parts. Before he found his real vocation, before the motion pictures claimed him as their great comedian, he trod the boards of the "legitimate" stage, and with no small success. He ran the theatrical gamut from minstrelsy to Shakespeare. Annie Russell, Maude Adams, Weber and Fields —these are a few of the stars whose radiance he augmented during the first twenty-five years of his professional life. But to-day the regular drama offers little opportunity to the true clown, and it was not until he appeared on the screen that John Bunny reach his own public—that is, the world.

The word clown has fallen of late years into unmerited disrepute. Impressionistic critics of the drama attempt to disparage a comedian by calling him a "mere clown." They might as well call Mr. Sargent a "mere painter," or M. Rodin a "mere sculptor." What they mean is that the comedian of their discontent is not a clown at all. For the grotesquely clad men, with whitened, expressionless faces, who tumble about the circus ring, have no right to the exclusive possession of their title. Indeed, few of them are genuine clowns in the best sense of the word, for most of them cause laughter by obvious horseplay, not by the true clown methods of elaborate pantomime and striking facial contortions.

The greatest comedians have been the greatest clowns. Even the most brilliant lines, spoken most winningly, fail of their effect upon the audience unless the speaker has a clown's power to act with his features. And if a clown be great enough he may safely dispense with words—as John Bunny did.

The English pantomime even in Thackeray's day had fallen from its once high place. The lovely Columbine remained and the sprightly Harlequin and the grotesque Pantaloon. But there were songs and dialogue; the entertainment was simply a sort of vaudeville, not genuine pantomime at all. It was not until the huge, clicking camera made lasting the gestures of the actors that the art of pantomime came back to its own.

There is a word used by men and women who have to do with this great branch of the world's amusement which deserves immortality. It is the verb "register." An actor registers grief, or amusement, or astonishment. That is, he assumes an expression which, when recorded by the camera and exhibited, will convey his emotion to the audience. In that one word there is a valuable treatise on the dramatic art. The inferior actor is content with expressing an emotion. The true actor registers it.

And what a sense of permanence is in that word "register!" Alfred de Musset and many another sentimental poet lamented the ephemeral nature of the actor's fame. The painter, it has been said, the writer and the sculptor, live in their works. But the actor's art perishes with him; when he dies, the memory of his expressive face and graceful form goes into the oblivion that keeps the echoes of his golden voice.

Well, we have changed all that. The number of people who lose their cares under the spell of John Bunny's magic to-day is greater than it was a year ago. The motion pictures have made the actor's chances for immortality equal with those of his fellows in the other arts.

Enemies of the motion picture (there really are such people) say that the humor of such entertainments is not true humor, but vulgar and barbarous horseplay, requiring no art. Anyone, they say, can get a laugh, as Charlie Chaplin does, by being knocked down by an automobile or by being grossly fat, like John Bunny.

The adequate answer to a critic who makes such statements as these is "Go out in the street and get knocked down by an automobile." This may be the remark which actors (and sensitive producers) commonly feel like making to dramatic critics, but in this case it should have no tinge of bitterness. Go out in the street and get knocked down by an automobile. See if the people laugh at you as they laugh at Chaplin. They will laugh at you only if you are artist enough to be knocked down humorously—as Chaplin is knocked down.

And, as to John Bunny's success being due to his fatness, that criticism is generally made by people who never saw "Autocrat of Flapjack Junction" or "Love's Old Dream," or by rival actors. It is true that your true clown always is quick to utilize his physical peculiarities as accessories to his acting. The jesters of Marie de Medici made fun of their own hunched backs or dwarfed forms. John Bunny had as good a right to turn his fatness into dramatic capital as Sarah Bernhardt has to do the same thing with her slenderness. It is a principle of subjective artistic expression—the same principle as that by which Heine made his little songs out of his great woes.

But the physical peculiarity alone is not enough. John Bunny was gifted by nature for his rôles. But he would have been a great clown even had he been built like John Drew. He would have made his shapeliness what he made his unshapeliness—something ridiculously amusing.

If fatness alone was the source of his success, how crowded his profession would now be! But this is not the case. Thousands, perhaps, of motion-picture audiences have watched Mr. Taft serenely cross the screen, or mutely seem to make a speech. Undoubtedly, they have thereby been edified. But they have not rocked from side to side with unextinguishable laughter, and thereafter burst into shouts of mirth at the mention of the ex-President's name.

No, people did not laugh at John Bunny because he was fat, or because he fell from horses and automobiles and aëroplanes, and submitted to various picturesque forms of assault and battery for their amusement. They laughed at him because he was fat humorously, because he fell from vehicles humorously, because he was a great clown—that is, a master of a difficult and important branch of dramatic art.

The motion-picture producers may not be aware of the fact, but they have performed a valuable service to the stage in reviving the art of pantomime. The actor in the spoken drama will be less likely to be a mere voice when he sees his brother on the screen act with his whole body.

Is it possible that the importance of the human voice has been exaggerated? Certainly the mechanical reproduction of the spoken word has not captured the world's attention as has the reproduction of motion. The phonograph, of course, brings the lovely notes of the singers to ears that otherwise would never thrill with melody. It has been used as an instrument by which a political speaker might address at one time twenty audiences scattered across the continent, and it has delighted with humorous dialogue those who were far from theaters. But as an interpreter of great literature, the needle revolves impotently upon its waxen cylinder.

There have been successful attempts to synchronize the phonograph and the motion-picture machine, to cause the words to accompany the action. It may be that these devices will one day be widely popular. But I hope not. For that would destroy the greatest value of motion-picture acting, the silent but complete expression of thought. The motion picture is the renascence of pantomime.

When Colley Cibber looked through his jeweled quizzing glass at a strange dumb-show drama newly

IN MEMORIAM: JOHN BUNNY

brought to England from merry France, a representation of the legend of Venus and Mars, he said that it was "form'd into a connected presentation of Dances in Character, wherein the Passions were so happily expressed, and the whole Story so intelligibly told, by a mute Narration of Gesture only, that even thinking Spectators allow'd it both a pleasing and rational Entertainment." It was this "pleasing and rational Entertainment" which developed into the great English pantomime, which popular custom (always fond of tradition and ritual) honored by association with the mighty festival of Christmas.

And the English pantomime's greater descendant is to be seen on many a modern film. Still the vivacious lover flees from the comic policemen and the irate father, still Columbine is fair, although she bears a less beautiful name and has changed her airy spangled draperies for a modern garb.

Why has no enterprising producer given us a real old English pantomime in the films, with all the conventional characters? What a Columbine Mary Pickford would make! And how excellently would Charles Chaplin's deft stumble suit Harlequin! There could be transformation scenes that would delight the genial ghosts of Lamb and

Thackeray. But who would be clown—now that John Bunny is dead?

The written word sometimes loses its power to bring laughter as the years roll by. Topical allusions, phrases, and sentiments that amuse us will bring no mirth to the hearts of our grandchildren. But there are certain things that are elementally funny, that make all people laugh who have any laughter in their souls. And one of these things is the face of John Bunny.

THE DAY AFTER CHRISTMAS

OF course, people still ride on the elevated **rail- ways**. But not the people who used to be taken over by their mothers from Jersey City on the Cortlandt Street Ferry about once every month, and then up Sixth Avenue by the elevated en route for the shops. These people now know the swift and monotonous tube train instead of the rakish ferryboat, the dull subway instead of the stimulating elevated railway. And even if they knelt upon the seats of the subway car, their rubbers projecting into the aisles and their faces pressed against the windows, they would see only blank walls and dismal stations instead of other people's Christmas trees.

These evanescent bits of glory lent special delight to aërial journeyings for weeks after Christmas. For, in defiance of the Twelfth Night convention, certain citizens were wont to keep their Christmas trees in place until February. And, in the opinion of the tenants of the third stories of the tenements (apartment houses is the more courteous word) which bordered the elevated, the place of the Christmas tree was close up against the front window, where all the world could enjoy its green and gold and red.

Like nearly all genuine vulgar customs (vulgar is used in its most honorable sense) this habit of showing the public the home's chief splendor was (or is, for undoubtedly firs dressed for holiday still brighten some lower Sixth Avenue windows) based on generous courtesy. It was not possible for Mr. Tenement to keep open flat, so to speak, at Christmas time; to summon all Sixth Avenue in to partake of a bowl of wassail that steamed upon his gas range. But he performed all the hospitality that his ungentle residence allowed; he placed his bit of greenwood with its cardboard angel, its red paper bells, and its strings of tinsel, where it would give to the greatest possible number the same delight that it gave to its owner.

It is, you observe, in your own psychological way, the Rogers Group principle. Your grandmother put "Going for the Cows," you remember, on the marble top of the walnut table by the window in the front parlor. The Nottingham lace curtains were parted just above the head of the boy who was urging the dog after the woodchuck.

And everybody who went up or down Maple Avenue got a good view of that masterpiece of realism. Therein your grandmother showed truer courtesy than did you when you put Rodin's "Le Baiser" in that niche above the second landing of your stairway.

The same quality of almost quixotic generosity is suggested by the composition of the old-fashioned holly wreaths, which, hung in the windows, showed to passers-by lustrous green leaves and scarlet berries, and to those who hung them only a circle of pale stems and wire. Even the lithographers maintain this courteous tradition; they stamp their cardboard holly wreaths on only one side. And this is the side which is to face the street.

Well, these fenestral firs and hollies exist, and they are among the numerous joys of the days that follow Christmas. These post-Christmas days shine with a light softer, but perhaps more comfortable, than that of the great feast itself.

Particularly is this true of the first day after Christmas—especially when that day is Sunday. In England, of course, as in the time of the late Samuel Pickwick, Esq., who brought about the renascence of Christmas, this is called Boxing Day, not because it is the occasion of fistic encounters, but because it is the time appointed for the distribution of those more or less spontaneous expressions of good will which are called Christmas boxes. Its more orthodox title is Saint Stephen's Day; it is, you know, the day on which the illustrious King Wenceslaus, with the assistance of his page, did his noble almoning. Says the old carol:

Good King Wenceslaus looked out
  On the feast of Stephen,
When the snow lay round about,
  Deep, and crisp, and even;
Brightly shone the moon that night,
  Though the frost was cruel;
When a poor man came in sight,
  Gathering winter fuel.

"Hither, page, and stand by me,
  See thou dost it telling
Yonder peasant, who is he,
  Where and what his dwelling?"
"Sire, he lives a good league hence,
  Underneath the mountain,
Over by the forest fence,
  By Saint Agnes fountain."

"Bring me flesh and bring me wine,
  Bring me pine logs hither;
Thou and I will see him dine,
  When we bear them thither."

THE DAY AFTER CHRISTMAS

Page and monarch forth they went,
  Forth they went together
Through the night wind's wild lament
  And the wintry weather.

We are not old English Kings, so instead of having our page bring flesh and wine to the poor man on Saint Stephen's Day, we give a dollar to the youth from the still vexed Bermuthes who chaperons the elevator in our apartment house, and for weeks before Christmas we affix to the flaps of the envelopes containing our letters little stamps bearing libelous caricatures of Saint Nicholas of Bari. Theoretically this last process provides a modicum of Christmas cheer for certain carefully selected and organized poor people.

However this may be, the fact remains that the day after Christmas is a very good day, indeed. The excitement of giving and receiving has passed away; there remains the quieter joy of contemplation. And since this year the day after Christmas is Sunday, this contemplation will not be disturbed by the arrival of the postman, who, a relentless bill-bringer, is, like the Greeks, to be feared even when bearing gifts.

And, in spite of the remarks of every humorist who ever borrowed from his mother-in-law two cents to put on an envelope which should carry a joke about her to an editor, this post-Christmas meditation nearly always is pleasant. It is assisted by the consumption of wife-bestowed cigars, which (again despite the humorists!) are better than those a man buys for himself. It is a pleasant meditation, for its subjects are things given and things received, good deeds done and good deeds experienced.

It also contains, this day-after-Christmas feeling, a quality of reconciliation. Not of reconciliation with ancient enemies—this was all orthodoxly attended to on Christmas Eve—but of reconciliation with affairs, of readjustment.

On Christmas Day there may have been some slight disappointment, some fly in the ointment, or, worse still, in the punch. Forgetting for a moment that you were just now pictured smoking cigars presented to you by your wife, let us consider you to be, as you probably are, a young woman of some eighteen Summers and perhaps an equal number of Winters. It is the day after Christmas; it is (although you are unaware of the fact) Saint Stephen's Day. Yesterday, although you endeavored to conceal the fact, only revealing it in the unnecessary viciousness with which you scrubbed the remains of a red and white striped candy basket from the countenance of your infant brother—yesterday, I repeat, you were annoyed. And the cause of your annoyance was that you received from the amorous Theophilus a paltry dozen, instead of twenty-four or thirty-six, American Beauties. Now, however, during your post-Christmas meditation, your annoyance is swept away by the refreshing thought that Theophilus will now have twelve or twenty-four dollars more to invest in that extraordinary solitaire diamond ring with which he purposes to decorate your not too reluctant hand as soon as people begin to see through your bluff of not being engaged. This thought cheers you considerably, and you dreamily give the aforesaid infant brother permission to consume a barley sugar elephant, which makes him very unwell.

Or, let us, on the other hand, suppose that you, who are now reading this inquiry into the theory of motives and ideas, are that infant brother himself. Your age, we will say, is three, and you are, we regret to say, somewhat sticky. Nevertheless, your frame of mind is, on the whole, more satisfactory than it was yesterday. You had in all confidence requested Santa Claus to bring you a large live baboon. Instead, he brought you a small tin monkey on a stick.

This was a genuine disappointment, as poignantly felt as will be any more obvious tragedy of your adult years. But, like all sorrows of childhood, it had the blessed quality of brevity. Now, on the day after Christmas, you contemplate with favor your tin monkey. One of his legs is broken, but he has come off his stick, and is therefore the more agreeable companion. Your father's apology for Santa Claus—to the effect that the baboon of your desire would have walked off with your stockings if he had been placed in them—seems reasonable. And there is manna for your soul in the thought that your father will take you to the Bronx Zoo this afternoon, and that you then can show your tin monkey to the baboon that lives there.

This peaceful meditation is one of the most delightfully comfortable features of the day after Christmas. This day has not the concentrated excitement of Christmas. It is, I think, the most restful day in the year. It is not marked, like January 2, with the shock of receiving bills and the strain of keeping new resolutions. It is a delightfully lazy day, a sort of sublimated Sunday afternoon.

And one conclusion which you should draw from your St. Stephen's Day meditation is that the nobility of Christmas traditions and customs is proved

[132]

by their surviving the most unfavorable, even absurd, conditions of life. It was not difficult for the Puritans to destroy the Maypole; its gay garlands never rose from the dust into which their iron heels trod them. But the Christmas tree—which even more than the Maypole was an idolatrous abomination to those of our forefathers who turned "the sword of the Lord and of Gideon" against the primitive red citizens of New England—the Christmas tree blooms with new splendor every year. It is set up even in the conventicle and New Salems which the Pilgrims established, and as its green branches glow with their precious freight of scarlet and gold, around it dance—tango, in fact—the descendants of John Alden and Priscilla Mullens.

But the Christmas tree and its attendant glories have survived an assault sterner than that of the Puritans. They are healthily surviving modern metropolitan conditions—the deadly foe of many gracious things. And the mere fact of survival is itself beautiful. It is very fine, of course, for Santa Claus to clamber down the broad chimney of a great farmhouse. But it is really noble of him to penetrate the mysterious smokestacks of a New York building, and, making some subtle use, I suppose, of the steam radiator, to visit every apartment which has its complement of childhood. It is admirable for a country child to believe in Santa Claus; but how much more admirable is the faith of the city child, the faith which stands the shock of the imitation Santa Clauses who strut about the department stores and beg at every corner!

These things, I said, are natural fruits of after-Christmas meditations. And the Christmas tree remains—although the gifts that surrounded it have been taken away, it is a pleasanter sight than it was yesterday, because it is already a beautiful old friend, a friend to whom we are grateful. It does not look ridiculous because its great day is gone, as, for example, a fire-cracker looks ridiculous on July 5. For Christmas is more than a day, it is a season, of which December 25 is only the commencement. And as the Christmas tree seems pleasanter and more friendly when some of its needles have formed little green aromatic heaps on the carpet, and when the china angel and two or three of the red glass balls have been taken down for the baby to play with—so does the Christmas season seem pleasanter and more friendly when its first great feast and pageant has come to its joyous close and become a part of time's rich treasury of golden days.

[134]

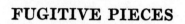

FUGITIVE PIECES

THE ASHMAN

PEOPLE

AN ASHMAN.
A POLICEMAN.
A LITTLE GIRL IN GREEN.

SCENE: *A city alley. The* ASHMAN *is fastening a nosebag on his horse, which is harnessed to a wagon half-filled with ashes. A* POLICEMAN *is watching him.*
TIME: *Noon.*

POLICEMAN
What do you feed him? Ashes?

ASHMAN
                  No, I don't!
I feed him Harps. Come over here, you boob,
And let him bite your face, he's hungry!

POLICEMAN
                  Aw!
You're nothing but a Harp yourself, you poor
Old God-forsaken ashman; Or a wop,
Or some fool kind of foreigner.

ASHMAN

O Hell!

You make me sick, you big fat pie-faced mutt!
Get out, you spoil my horse's appetite!

POLICEMAN

I'd hate to be your horse, but then I guess
I'd rather be your horse than you.   (*Exit.*)

(*A* LITTLE GIRL IN GREEN *appears from behind the wagon.*)

LITTLE GIRL

Hello!

ASHMAN

Hello there, kiddo!   Where did *you* come from?
(*Climbs to his seat on the wagon, takes out a tin pail, and begins to eat his lunch.*)

LITTLE GIRL

I think I'd like some bread and butter, please!

ASHMAN

All right, old girl, just take a bite of that.
(*Tosses his half loaf down to her.*)

LITTLE GIRL

There isn't any butter on it.

ASHMAN

No.

I haven't got no butter.   But it's good,

[138]

It's first-rate bread, all right.

LITTLE GIRL (*tossing back the loaf, from which she
has taken a bite*)
   Thanks very much! Thanks, Captain Thunder!

ASHMAN
                        Huh?
You're a queer kid, all right, and hungry, too,
To eat dry bread. (*Eats some of the bread.*) Why
      damn my eyes! God's wounds!
Here's scurvy provender. (*Throws the bread
      down.*) And scurvy mirth!
What, Kate! Dear Kate o' the Green, well met,
      well met,
Slip up and sit beside me, lass! It's not
The first time you have been upon this seat.

LITTLE GIRL (*climbing up beside him*)
No, Captain, I should know the Royal Mail,
But when did you take up the coaching trade?
I had as soon expect to see old Dick
Throw leg across your Monmouth's gleaming back,
Thrust pistols in his belt, and gallop off
To make his fortune in the light o' the moon,
As to find you, the Master of the Heath,
The Devil's Treasurer, the Velvet Mask,
The Silver Pistoleer, the Wingèd Thief,

Sitting with down-cast Sabbath-keeping eyes,
Sad lips, and nose all fixed for droning psalms,
In old Dick's place upon the Royal Mail.
A proper driver for a coach and four!

ASHMAN

Ha' done! God's mercy on us! Let me speak,
And I will tell you such a waggery
Will make you laugh and split your pretty sides:
I stole the Royal Mail!

LITTLE GIRL

You stole the Mail?

ASHMAN

Aye, prigged it, Kate! Why, here it is, you see,
Box, boot and wheels, four horses and a whip,
And on the door King George's coat of arms.
All mine, good lass, all mine. But for a price,
A bitter price, dear Kate. For Monmouth's dead!

LITTLE GIRL

What, Monmouth, best of horses, is he dead?
O Captain Thunder, never tell me that!
Why, all the world holds not another horse
So glossy black, so fleet, so wise, so kind!

ASHMAN

Yes, Monmouth's dead. Dick shot him through the
    heart,

And Monmouth dropped without a whinny. But
I paid Dick back. O Monmouth is avenged!
Now, hear me, Kate! I stopped the Royal Mail
Last night at twelve o'clock at Carter's Cross,
Says I, "Stand now! And let me have the bags—
That's all I want to-night! Hand over, there!"
Dick pulls his leaders on their haunches. "Why,"
Says he, "it's Captain Thunder! By my wig!
Just help yourself!" I prigged his pistol belt
And rode around to look inside the coach.
I got the bags. The passengers were three.
My Lord of Bath and Wells—

LITTLE GIRL

A Bishop, what?

ASHMAN

Aye, that he is; white wig and bands and all.
Yes, he's a Bishop. And there was his wife,
(A big fat monster of a wife) and then
There was a little wizened-looking thing,
A sort of curate. Well, I looked at them
And laughed to see them tremble in their shoes.
"Good e'en, my Lord," says I, and doffed my hat.
"How do you like the Royal Mail?" Says he:
"O good Sir Highwayman, pray let me go,
Our coach broke down at York, and so we took
This public carrier, this dreadful thing,

This Royal Mail. O will you let us pass?
I must get into Hull by dawn, and sleep,
For I confirm an hundred souls at noon."
I listened to him, Kate, and did not see
The old fox slip a pistol up to Dick.
But, bang! Hell's fury! Down fell Monmouth,
       dead.
And off I stumbled in the ditch! Well, Kate,
Dick aimed for me, you see, and got the horse.
And I got Dick. I got him through the head.
And then I joined the Bishop once again.
"Come out, my Lord, and strip!" says I. "What,
      strip?"
Says he, and let his jaw fall on his chest.
"Yes, strip!" says I, and pulls his great-coat off:
"Yes, strip!" says I, and throws his wig away:
"Yes, strip!" says I, and pulls his breeches off:
And there he stands and shivers, pink and fat.
"Now, Madame Bishopess," says I, "pray do
Poor Captain Thunder so much courtesy
As to ride by him on the way to town."
She screamed and fought. I took her in my arms
And heaved her up into the seat. "Now strip!"
I shouted to the curate. "Yes," says he,
"I'll strip," and strip he did. "Inside!" says I;
They stumbled headlong in, I cracked my whip

THE ASHMAN

And, whoop! the Mail went rumbling on to Hull!
Well, just at dawn we passed the Southern Gate;
We galloped down the street and made a halt
Beside the Close. "Here's the Cathedral, dame!"
Says I, and helped the lady to the ground.
"Unbar the door, and help his Lordship out
And don't forget the curate!" How I laughed
To see the Bishop and the curate run
Stark naked, screaming, to the Chapter House!
Well, I was off at once and out of Hull
And never stopped to breathe the nags till now.

LITTLE GIRL

But, Captain Thunder! Captain! Are you mad?
They'll have the country after you! Be quick!
You can't make cover in a coach and four
As on a horse! ### ASHMAN

Nay, Kate, rest easy now.
Red Will is out, and Davy Doublesword,
And Hieland Jock, and Dan the Drum and Ned,
And twenty gallant gentlemen beside.
And they have sworn to keep the roadway clear
By setting all the lobsters such a chase
Will scatter them till night. And Ned will blow
His bugle when the way is safe. Then, whoop!
I'll rattle off again and fill the coach

With gentlemen of fortune, comrades true,
And own the road from here to London town.

(*A horn is heard and a cry of* "Fish, fish, fish, fine fresh fish!")

LITTLE GIRL

Down, Captain, loose the horses! There's the call!

(*The* ASHMAN *gets down, takes off the horse's nosebag and unhitches the horse from the post.*)

ASHMAN (*getting back on his seat*)

Now, Kate, we'll gallop off to Arcady.

POLICEMAN (*suddenly entering*)

Hello there, Ashes, who you talking to?

ASHMAN

Kate of the Greenwood.

POLICEMAN

Kate? You poor old boob!
You're crazy in the head. There's no one there!

ASHMAN (*driving off*)

Make way there, constable. (*Cracks his whip and sings.*)

Come all ye jolly rovers
As wants to hear a tale
Will make your hearts as merry
As a bellyful of ale.

[144]

THE ASHMAN

I'll sing of Captain Thunder,
　　And his dashing slashing way,
How he kissed the queen and he cuffed the
　　king,
　　And threw the crown away!

(Exit)

POLICEMAN

Well, I'll be damned!

THE BEAR THAT WALKS LIKE A MAN

IT would be a relief to meet a man who would tell honestly why he likes Artzibashev and some of the rest of the modern Russian realists. It would be a relief to have some young radical say: "Yes, I know Chekhov is dull and prolix, but then the atmosphere of his work is delightfully unwholesome, and every now and then there is something pleasantly morbid, like the man with phosphorous poisoning in 'The Steppe,' and his agreeable custom of eating live fish. And then there's dear Michael Artzibashev. Of course his style is no better than that of Laura Jean Libbey, and his plots are cheap melodrama, but you can't deny that he is consistently nasty. And I do like to read about sexual depravity."

But the young radical of this sort is hard to meet. Instead we find the lofty-foreheaded young man who praises Artzibashev's psychological insight, Gorky's sympathy with humanity, and—actually! —Chekhov's humor! Of course he does not mean what he says. He likes "Sanine" for the same

[146]

reason that he likes "Three Weeks." But he would not dare to confess a liking for "Three Weeks" because that book is English trash. And "Sanine" is Russian trash. And from the point of view of intellectual snobbery, there's all the difference in the world between these two sorts of trash.

Now, it would of course be absurd to condemn all modern Russian fiction, or to characterize all admirers of contemporary Russian novelists as hypocrites and sensualists. Americans and Englishmen who know almost by heart the great poems and stories of Pushkin, who know Lermóntov as they know Byron, and Gogol as they know Dickens, who were brought up on the novels of Turgenieff, have every right in the world to seek for new delight among the outpourings of the presses of Petrograd and Moscow. But the sort of person who is feverishly enthusiastic over Gorky and Artzibashev has discovered Russian literature, in all probability, during the few years which have passed since his graduation from Harvard. His most serious offense is not that he prefers that which is evil to that which is good, and praises untrue and inartistic work because the worst part of his nature responds to its salacious appeal. His most serious offense is that he thinks that the Hall

Caines and Marie Corellis of Russia really are representative writers, and that he insults a race of great romanticists and great realists by calling works that are thoroughly morbid and vile "very Russian."

What is the remedy for this unfortunate condition? The ideal course to pursue would be, of course, to spank the serious-minded young men who think that the Russian novel is a cross between Nijinsky's dancing and a pogrom. They should be sentenced to a year in solitary confinement, during which they should be obliged to read daily a very thoroughly expurgated edition of all Artzibashev's works. This would convince them that it was not Artzibashev's "power of psychological analysis" that attracted them, and they would return to the world sadder and more honest men.

But this most desirable course has not the virtue of practicality. Perhaps some of the more or less recent activities of American publishers will so educate the public that they will no longer be impressed by critics whose acquaintance with Russian literature is confined to "Sanine" and some of Gorky's plays. Not long ago was published Stephen Graham's admirable translation of Gogol's "Dead Souls," a novel which in its rich humor and sympathetic realism suggests "Pickwick Papers," while its whimsical romanticism brings to mind some parts of "Don Quixote." It is one of the world's classics; no one who has not read it has a right to an opinion on Russian literature. About the same time appeared Tolstoy's "The Death of Ivan Ilyitch," a book of short stories by the great novelist, half genius and half mountebank, who wasted his genuine talent in developing a new religion, which is merely a grotesque parody of Christianity. The stories in this book are compelling, in spite of their somewhat mad philosophy, for they faithfully reflect Russian manners and certain picturesque phases of Russian idealism. Another volume issued at about this period is Maurice Baring's "Russian Literature," the best one-volume work on the subject in existence. And it is to be hoped that other publishers will publish those Russian novels which really belong to literature, rather than those which are of interest chiefly to the pathologist and alienist.

But meanwhile the market is flooded with viciously sensational works which are tolerated only because their exotic quality gives them a certain distinction in the eyes of the provincial. Here, for example, is Maxim Gorky's "Submerged." Mr.

Jerome's "The Passing of the Third Floor Back," and Charles Rand Kennedy's "The Servant in the House" were sentimental, but on the whole, effective treatments of a very dangerous theme: that of the miraculous reformation of certain phases of modern society or groups of individuals through the appearance on earth of a man possessing Divine attributes. Gorky's plan has a similar plot, but, of course, he differs from the two English writers in making vice triumph in the end. The poor wretches who have endeavored to regain a little of their lost decency are thrust back into the slime. The people who make up this typical Gorky offering are drunkards, thieves, depraved creatures of every kind. They are utterly lost and the author seems to gloat over their depravity and misery. But then what else is he to do? He must live up to his name. Gorky, you know, is a pen name meaning "bitter," and Alexei Maximovitch Pyeshkov feels that he must justify the title he has so proudly assumed. But ridiculous affectation it is! It is as if Matthew Arnold had called himself "Matthew Sweetness and Light."

And there is a translation of Leonidas Andreiev, "The Red Laugh." This was an attempt to flash upon the astonished world the novel idea that war

is a very, very unpleasant thing. Mr. Andreiev
spills gore on every page, and the publisher assists
him by making the title of the book blood red on a
black ground. All the characters in the book go
mad, and the author's utter inaptitude for literature
turns what might have been passable third-rate
melodrama into a farce. As a contribution to letters, and as a piece of pacifist propaganda "The
Red Laugh" is inferior to "I Didn't Raise My Boy
to Be a Soldier."

And then there is Artzibashev: so much boomed
and press-agented; praised by the radical magazines
for his "assault on ordinary morality" and his "desperately poignant artistry"; long-haired young
men with large eyes have told the women's clubs all
about him. Well, of course, "desperately poignant
artistry" means nothing at all, and "artistry" is
meaningless when used in connection with a man
like the author of "The Millionaire." He doesn't
write novels, he merely throws something evil-
smelling into the reader's face.

If the scene of "The Millionaire" and "Nina"
were laid in the United States, these stories would
never have been printed. They are without literary
merit; they are the crudest melodrama, but their
grossness makes them appeal to the prurient, and

their foreign origin charms the literary snob. To say that they reflect Russian life is to insult Russia grievously. They do reflect, it is true, the basest part of Russian life, the part which no friend of Russia or of literature can wish reflected. They reflect the gross and hideous bestiality of the Russian criminal class, they reflect the life of people who have added to their native savagery the vices of civilization. They call to mind a picture of the Russian people as something at once bestial and human, a monstrosity, a nightmare: perhaps the thing that Kipling had in mind when he wrote of the bear that walks like a man.

ABSINTHE AT THE CHESHIRE
CHEESE

BELONGING rather to gossip than to literary history, the following anecdote is nevertheless significant when considered merely as an illustrative legend. A certain London publisher, it is said, recently had in his possession a notebook that had been found, after his death, among the effects of Lionel Johnson. The poet had scribbled in it memoranda of all sorts: notes for essays, stray epigrams, rough drafts of poems. He had also copied into it, from books and magazines, bits of prose and verse that gave him pleasure. Well, one day this friend said to Johnson's loyal friend, Miss Louise Imogen Guiney—and, by the way, Miss Guiney is not my authority for this story—"Do you know, I have found in this notebook an unpublished poem by Lionel Johnson! It is very beautiful, far better than any of Johnson's published poems. I'll read it to you." Thereupon he opened the notebook and began to declaim:

FUGITIVE PIECES

Last night, ah, yesternight, between her lips and
     mine
There fell thy shadow, Cynara!

Of course Lionel Johnson, like every other lover
of good poetry, had felt the charm of Ernest Dowson's now famous poem which is headed by the
phrase, "Non Sum Qualis Eram Bonæ Sub Regno
Cynaræ," and had hastily copied it in his notebook,
perhaps from Dowson's manuscript at some meet-
ing of the Rhymers' Club. The point of this story
is that the publisher, knowing Johnson chiefly as
a celebrant of the Catholic faith, attributed to him
not one of Dowson's poems about nuns, or Extreme
Unction, or the Blessed Sacrament, but a lyric
which at least in tradition and phrasing is obviously
pagan.

Out of the mouths of babes and publishers! That
wise and sympathetic critic, Miss Katherine Brégy,
has justly praised the lovely poetry which resulted
from Ernest Dowson's return to the faith of his
ancestors. She has demonstrated, for all time, the
genuineness of his Catholicism, and made Mr. Victor Plarr's recent sneer at his dead friend's conversion seem the most futile thing in his entertaining
but ineffective book. It would be absurd for me

[154]

to attempt to add to Miss Brégy's interpretative appreciations of the "sculptural beauty" of Dowson's religious poems. But, like the simple-minded publisher previously mentioned, I find indications, if not of piety, at least of normality, sanity, wholesomeness, virtue, in nearly every poem which this so-called "decadent" wrote.

There are, and there have always been since sin first came into the world, genuine "decadents." That is, there have been writers who have devoted all their energies and talents to the cause of evil, who have consistently and sincerely opposed Christian morality, and zealously endeavored to make the worse appear the better cause. But every poet who lays a lyric wreath at a heathen shrine, who sings the delights of immorality, or hashish, or suicide, or mayhem, is not a decadent: often he is merely weak-minded. The true decadent, to paraphrase a famous saying, wears his vices lightly, like a flower. He really succeeds in making vice seem picturesque and amusing and even attractive.

Now, this is exactly what Ernest Dowson never could do. He was a member, it will be remembered, of that little band of "esthetic" poets which was called the Rhymers' Club. With them he spent certain evenings at the Cheshire Cheese and there he drank absinthe. This is a significant and symbolic fact. Not in some ominous Parisian cellar, but beneath the beamed ceiling of a most British inn, still stained with smoke from the pipe of Dr. Samuel Johnson, among thick mutton chops and tankards of musty ale, in a cloud of sweet-scented steam that rose from the parted crust of the magnificent pigeon-pie, Ernest Dowson drank absinthe.

Of course it is true—more's the pity!—that in the melancholy years just before his death he drank absinthe in places where it is terribly fitting to drink absinthe. But this does not destroy the splendid symbolism of his act of drinking absinthe in the Cheshire Cheese. The wickedness in his poems and in his prose-sketches are always as affected and incongruous as is that pallid medicine in any honest tavern.

He tried hard to be pagan. In the manner of Mr. Swinburne, he exclaimed: "Goddess the laughter-loving, Aphrodite, befriend! Let me have peace of thee, truce of thee, golden one, send!" And not even Mr. Swinburne ever wrote lines so absolutely unconvincing. He said, "I go where the wind blows, Chloe, and am not sorry at all." And from this lyric no one can fail to get the impression that the poet was very sorry indeed. He imitated, even less successfully than Oscar Wilde, the unpleasant prose poems of Baudelaire, and he made the very worst of all English versions of Paul Verlaine's "Colloque Sentimental."

When Dowson took hashish during his student days, Mr. Arthur Symons tells us, it was before a large and festive company of friends. I do not think that he convinced them that he was that supposedly romantic character, an habitual user of the drug. The hashish, so to speak, in his poems is similarly incongruous and unconvincing. He was an accomplished artist in words, a delicate, sensitive and graceful genius, but he was no more fitted to be a pagan than to be a policeman. And so, in his best-known poem, he uses all the pagan properties, all the splendors of sin's pageantry, but his theme, his over-mastering thought—very different from the over-mastering thought of, say, Mr. Arthur Symons in similar circumstances—is a soul-shaking lament for his stained faithfulness, for his treason to the Catholic ideal of chastity.

He could not write poems that really were pagan. He was not a true decadent. And for this undoubtedly he now is thanking God. He had his foolish hours: he sometimes misused his gift of song. But—and this is the important thing about it—he did not know how to misuse it successfully. The real Ernest Dowson was not the picturesque vagabond about whom Mr. Arthur Symons and Mr. Victor Plarr have written, but the man who with all his heart praised "meekness and vigilance and chastity," who "was faithful" in his pathetic, ineffective fashion, but who knew at least the fidelity of his eternal Mother, who, in Miss Brégy's beautiful words, "laid his broken body in consecrated ground and followed this bruised soul with her pitiful, asperging prayers."

JAPANESE LACQUER

WHAT was the matter with Lafcadio Hearn?
No American has written prose more delicate and vividly beautiful than his, nor has any one else—not even Yone Noguchi—put into English so clear a revelation of Japan's soul. Yet after an hour with "Kwaidan" or "Glimpses of Unfamiliar Japan" the normal reader is wearied and, instead of being grateful to the erudite and skillful author, regards him with actual dislike.

Why is this? Is it because Hearn had a morbid fondness for the tragic, and loved to dwell on mental, physical and spiritual disease? This is partly the reason, yet De Quincey and Edgar Allan Poe inspire no such aversion. Is it because Hearn's style is too rich, exquisite and precious? Walter Pater had the same fault, but Walter Pater is read with delight by Hearn's enemies. Is it because of Hearn's ridiculous religious prejudices—his hatred for the Jesuits, for example? No, Hearn's hatred for the Jesuits is simply a bad little boy's impudence toward his schoolmaster. He had none of

George Borrow's fiery, romantic passion against the "Man in Black." And Borrow's "Lavengro" and "Romany Rye" were loved even by so un-Protestant a writer as Lionel Johnson.

No, the reason lies deeper, and is simpler, than any of these. Hearn failed, not because he was precious, not because he was morbid, not because he was prejudiced, but because he had no imagination.

Lafcadio Hearn was, in the worst sense of the word, a realist. He had thoroughly the material-istic attitude toward life; he could see only the dull outside of things, not the indwelling splendor. An imaginative man would have delighted in his mixed Greek and Irish blood, would have realized that as a newspaperman he was a member of the most ro-mantic profession the world has known, would have seen that New Orleans was no mean city. But Hearn was so prosaic and matter-of-fact that he saw only the forms and outlines of the things about him, and so sentimentally credulous that he believed that Japan contained greater wonders than Louis-iana. Dr. George M. Gould, in his interesting but unpleasant work, "Concerning Lafcadio Hearn," blames many of his dead friend's faults on his de-

fective vision. But Hearn's myopia was spiritual
as well as physical: he could not see the soul.

What terrible results came from this spiritual
myopia! Of course, its worst result was the un-
speakable tragedy of Hearn's rejection of Christianity for that cruel burlesque on religion called
Buddhism. But the minor results were many and
dreadful . . . chief among them was the loss to the
world of a great writer.

Lafcadio Hearn might have been a great writer.
If proof of this were needed, it would be found in
a posthumously published book of singular interest—"Fantastics and Other Fancies." This is a
collection of Hearn's earliest writings, resurrected
from the brittle yellow pages of old New Orleans
newspapers by Charles Woodward Hutson.

The brief essays in this book are as charmingly
phrased as anything this master of charming
phrases ever wrote, and they are—unlike his later
work—imaginative. That is, they are interpretations and idealizations of the things naturally familiar to Hearn. He had not yet committed the
artistic heresy of confusing strangeness with
beauty. He was not yet deluded into the belief
that romance belongs exclusively to Nippon. He

still was loyal to the traditions of his own civilization.

The literary value of Hearn's work is not to be
questioned. No living writer (not even Algernon
Blackwood) has so great and fiery an imagination
as had this quondam reporter of the New Orleans
Daily Item; no living writer (except Alice Meynell) understands so thoroughly the art of putting
together a few hundred words so as to form a structure of enduring loveliness.

It was in 1878 that Lafcadio Hearn, half starved
and dressed in rags, persuaded Colonel John W.
Fairfax, owner of the New Orleans *Item,* to give
him work. He was called "assistant editor," but
it may be supposed that the "assistant editor" of
this little two-page paper did most of the repor-
torial work. What treasures of glowing narrative
its news columns may hold can only be conjectured.
But on its editorial page appeared from time to
time for several years brief sketches, some whimsical, some sombre, all highly imaginative and beautifully phrased. These, with other writings which
Hearn contributed later to the New Orleans
Times-Democrat, Dr. Hutson has searched out and
brought together in this volume of real charm and
value.

Any trivial incident of his daily round, any quaint bit of history or legend that he came upon in his amazingly extensive reading, would furnish this strangest of newspaper men with a theme. He saw in some antique shop a faun and dryad pictured in enamel on a little golden case, and, sitting at his littered, ink-stained desk in his noisy office, he wrote the exquisite "Idyl of a French Snuffbox." Riding to work in a clanging street car, he found on its floor a Japanese fan of paper, and wrote of its unknown owner with a gay fervor surprising in such an amateur of grief. Mark Twain came to New Orleans, and the result was that masterpiece of vivid and sympathetic description, "A River Reverie."

He was not always absolutely original, this obscure hack whose genius was one day to surprise and delight the world. Subconsciously, he remembered his spiritual brother, Edgar Allan Poe, when he wrote those tales of the grotesque and arabesque, "The Black Cupid" and "The One Pill Box." Also there are echoes of Coleridge, and of those Parnassian Frenchmen whose methods and ideals Hearn always shared.

But no Frenchman of his time could match the tender humor of "The Post Office," nor were Poe and Coleridge standing at his elbow when he wrote "Hiouen-Thrang." These were written by Lafcadio Hearn himself, by that strange nomad who called no one race his own, who looked at life with huge and perilous curiosity, who gave to most un-English thoughts a splendidly English dress, who just missed being a poet, who just missed being a mystic, who just missed being happy.

Already, the "Fantastics" show, Hearn was hearing the Orient's alluring voice. New Orleans, that brave old bright-colored Latin city, struggling with the aftermath of war and pestilence, was just the place for a man of his exotic tastes. "I cannot say how fair and rich and beautiful this dead South is," he wrote. "It has fascinated me." But not the venerable splendors of New Orleans, not the picturesque shores of Grand Isle, could take the place of the radiant East, to which he continually referred, of which clairvoyantly he seemed to know himself already a citizen.

There are sketches in this extraordinary little book, notably "Les Coulisses" and "The Undying One," which remind the reader, strangely enough, of certain prose fancies of another son of Ushaw, Francis Thompson. A healthier Lafcadio Hearn, with a broader vision and a tradition more clearly

English, might have written "Finis Coronat Opus."
And the thought makes one, perhaps, a little regretful that Hearn was so sincerely a gypsy, that
he was drawn away from the scenes of his young
manhood to a lovely but wholly alien land. Of
course, he wrote beautifully of Japan. But these
youthful sketches show that Japan was not necessary to his artistic expression. And to take on that
strange new culture he had to give up some heritages of thought and belief that he could ill spare, the
loss of which, it may be, is the cause of that melancholy, shading sometimes into despair, which permeates even his richest and most sympathetic
Japanese studies.

Hearn did not ruin himself as a writer by writing
about Japan. He ruined himself by trying to be
a Japanese. Now, one can write about Japan without being a Japanese, just as one can write about
hell without being damned. But Hearn was not
sufficiently imaginative to perceive this.

So he gave up European civilization for that of
Japan. His Irish father's faith held all that was
noble of his Greek mother's pagan tradition, but
Hearn chose the novelties of Buddhism. He went
to Japan: he devoted the gifts that God had given
him, and the technical skill that the Jesuits had

taught him, to the celebration of anti-Christian legends and ceremonials. But cherry-blossoms bloom only for a season—unlike Sharon's rose. And the tragic letters published after Hearn's death show that this fantastic adventurer learned at last that he had forsaken the splendid adventure first appointed for him. His bitter revilings of the people and customs of the land he had spent years in praising show that within Nippon's golden apples, too, are ashes.

Hearn has been held up by the sentimentalists as a shining example of humanity's cruelty to great artists. He is instead a shining example of the minor artist's cruelty to humanity. He was not rejected of men. His was not "divine discontent," his was the pernicious "desire for new things." Therefore he became merely the maker of fair and futile decorations, and he who might have been a poet, a creator, became a clever wordsmith.

The essays in this little book of Hearn's earliest work show a strange resemblance to the prose of Francis Thompson. What a contrast the lives of the two men present! Both were vagabonds, both were physically handicapped. But Francis Thompson was imaginative enough to be himself, so he wrote "The Hound of Heaven." And Lafcadio Hearn was so lacking in imagination as to want to be somebody else—so he wrote "Gleanings in Buddha Fields."

It is not for a mere journalist to point out the moral significance of the tragedy of Lafcadio Hearn. But I venture to suggest that the young American and English poets who are kissing the silken hem of Mr. Rabindranath Tagore's garment might profitably read Lafcadio Hearn's later correspondence. Fame and happiness are not always the reward of him who gives up the Occident for the Orient. Orientalism has its own truths, its own splendors. But the writers whose words we cherish, whose names are graven on our hearts, the makers of our literature, did anyone of these sell his birthright for a mess of—rice?

SAPPHO REDIVIVA

OUT of the dust of Egypt comes the voice of Sappho, as clear and sweet as when she sang in Lesbos by the sea, 600 years before the birth of Christ. The picks and spades of Arab workmen, directed by Bernard P. Grenfell and Arthur S. Hunt of the Egypt Exploration Fund, have given the world a hitherto unknown poem by the greatest woman poet of all time.

Of course it is not a complete and legible manuscript, this buried treasure unearthed at sunburnt Oxyrhyncus. It is a little pile of fragments of papyrus, fifty-six in all. And on one of them is the tantalizing inscription, "The First Book of the Lyrics of Sappho, 1,332 lines."

To piece these fragments together has been a task more delicate and arduous than to dig them out of the earth. Messrs. Grenfell and Hunt succeeded in combining some twenty shreds of papyrus, and thus in showing the nature of the original manuscript. And the chief product of their labor and skill was a poem of six stanzas in the form to which

SAPPHO REDIVIVA

Sappho's name is given, a poem, however, from which two entire lines and many words were missing.

Then it was that J. M. Edmonds, an eminent Hellenist of Cambridge University, gave his attention to the matter. He studied the possible relationship of the words, parsing and analyzing as diligently as any youth whom only the implacable Homer separates from a strip of parchment marked with the university's seal and his own name parodied in Latin.

"Anactoria," he saw, was vocative—and that was greatly significant. He added accents, syllables, words, and finally he supplied—it was pure guesswork, of course—two entire lines. And the result is undoubtedly a close approximation of the original lyric, more nearly complete, indeed, than most of the poems which have made critics call Sappho "the Tenth Muse."

For Sappho is known only by two brief odes and a few lyric fragments—"two small brilliants and a handful of star dust," they have been called. She wrote, it is believed, at least nine books of odes, together with epithalamia, epigrams, elegies, and monodies.

To account for the disappearance of all this

poetry several theories have been advanced. One, which is largely accepted, is that Sappho's poems were burned at Byzantium in the year A. D. 380 by command of Gregory Nazianzen, who desired that his own poems might be studied in their stead, for the improvement of the morals of his people.

J. M. Edmonds has contributed to an issue of *The Classical Review* his amended version of the poem. He gives also the following prose translation:

The fairest thing in all the world some say is a host of horsemen, and some a host of foot, and some, again, a navy of ships; but to me, 'tis my heart's beloved, and 'tis easy to make this understood by any.

When Helen surveyed much mortal beauty, she chose for the best the destroyer of all the honor of Troy, and thought not so much either of child or parent dear, but was led astray by love to bestow her heart afar; for woman is ever easy to be bent when she thinks lightly of what is near and dear.

Even so you to-day, my Anactoria, remember not, it seems, when she is with you one of whom I would rather have the sweet sound of her footfall and the sight of the brightness of her beaming face than all the chariots and armored footmen of Lydia.

Know that in this world man cannot have the

best; yet to pray for a share in what was once shared is better than to forget it.

I have roughly rendered the poem into English verse as follows:

Unto some a troop of triumphant horsemen,
Or a radiant fleet, or a marching legion,
Is the fairest sight—but to me the fairest
      Is my beloved.

Every lover must understand my wisdom,
For when Helen looked on the whole world's
      beauty
What she chose as best was a man, her loved one,
      Who shamed Troy's honor.

Then her little child was to her as nothing.
Not her mother's tears nor her father's pleading
Moved her. At Love's word, meekly she surren-
      dered
      Unto this stranger.

So does woman yield, valuing but little
Things, however fair, that she looks at daily.
So you now, Anactoria, forget her,
      Her, who is with you,

Her, to see whose face, fairer than the sunlight,
Her, to hear whose step ringing on the threshold,
I'd forego the sight of the Lydian army,
      Bowmen and chariots.

Never in this world is the best our portion,
Yet there is a vague pleasure in remembrance,
And to long for joy that has passed is better
    Than to forget it.

No one would venture to criticize Mr. Edmonds's treatment of the Greek text; his ingenious additions are a distinguished, scholarly achievement. Nor can any fault be found with his prose translation of the poem. But to readers of poetry who have not that peculiar literal-mindedness which characterizes scholars his interpretation of the translated poem, his explanation of Sappho's meaning, is anything but satisfactory.

It gives "point" to the piece, he says, if we imagine Anactoria to have fallen in love with a soldier. Sappho, he explains, clearly is away in exile. Anactoria and the other woman are living in the same town, presumably Mitylene. He gives this interpretation of Sappho's supposed address to Anactoria:

You, who are lucky enough to be with her still, have forgotten, it seems, a friend whom I would give anything to see again. For you have fallen in love. And yet it is natural enough; and I cannot blame you. But O, that I might have the joy you are throwing away! I know it is no use wishing;

but still, past delights are better missed than forgotten.

Now, it is the scholars that have brought the poets into disrepute. They insist on interpreting them and in being at once too literal and too imaginative. Take, for instance, the obvious example of Shakespeare. Plays and poems written for the entertainment of the world have been twisted and tortured by erudite commentators who have seen in them supernatural prophecies, scientific treatises, political tracts, and—what is in this connection especially important—personal confessions. Mankind cannot be restrained, it seems, from the attempt to interpret all poetry as rhymed autobiography.

Why, it is respectfully asked, does it give "point to the piece" to imagine that Anactoria has fallen in love with a soldier? Why drag in the soldier? Surely a poet may mention the panoply of war without having in mind any particular fighting man. The poem is simple and direct; it may be taken at its face value without the addition of any love affair other than that which primarily it celebrates.

Mr. Edmonds is, it may be objected, too imaginative when he supplies Anactoria with a mysterious military lover. He is perhaps too literal minded in the very essence of his interpretation. Strangely enough, he seems for the moment to forget that a poet is not compelled always to speak in propria persona.

Why should we believe that Sappho meant this poem as a personal message to a friend named Anactoria? Why is it not possible—even probable— that Sappho meant the poem as the utterance of someone else, of someone who existed only in her own splendid imagination?

If this were so the case would really not be without precedent. "My mother bore me in the southern wild; And I am black, but O, my soul is white," was not (as scholars of A. D. 2,000 may gravely state) the outcry of a little colored boy, but the work of an elderly English gentleman. Walter Savage Landor's "Mother, I Cannot Mind My Wheel," was not a personal expression—Mr. Landor, as his mother was well aware, had no wheel to mind. Shelley was not the daughter of Earth and Water and Browning never choked a young woman named Porphyria with her own hair.

No, in spite of the excellent advice that has been given them, poets refuse to look exclusively into their own hearts and write. They refuse to be consistently subjective, they insist on voicing the thoughts of others. Therefore, not all the scholars in Christendom and heathenry need keep us from regarding Sappho's newly found poem as anything but what, on the surface, it appears to be, the address of a rejected lover to a friend or sister of his lady.

If Mr. Edmonds's admirable prose translation be regarded in this light—which surely is the light of nature—what is there about it to perplex? That Sappho used the name "Anactoria" in other poems does not prove that in that shadowy school on Lesbos there was a girl so named. It is a good rhythmical name, fitting excellently into the middle of a lesser Sapphic strophe; why should not Sappho use it? Was Pompilia among Browning's acquaintances, or does E. A. Robinson write letters to Fleming Helphenstine and Minniver Cheevy?

Even if, because of the ode which Longinus praised and because of other references, we believe that Sappho really had an Anactoria among her friends or pupils, we are under no obligation to believe that this poem was meant for her. Leigh Hunt—not to speak of Rossetti!—knew many Jennies, but none of them ever sued him for libel.

Sappho, whom a contemporary called "the flower of the Graces," suffered first from her enemies and then from her friends. That "small, dark woman" who wrote immortal lyrics and counted among her disciples such famous singers as Erinna of Telos and Damophyla of Pamphylia, was, after her death, grossly calumniated by the ribald writers of Athenian comedy. Those who believe in the anecdotes of her which fill those scurrilous but entertaining pages cannot consistently refuse to credit also Aristophanes's interpretation of the character of Socrates.

If we are to take any of Sappho's poems as genuine personal expressions, certainly we cannot pass by her ode to her brother Charaxus, in which, in the most strict, not to say puritanical, fashion she rebukes him for yielding to the charms of the courtesan Doricha.

Nor can her correspondence with that Alceus, that "fluent poet of fluctuating moods," as E. B. Osborn calls him, be neglected. Alceus wrote to her, in an ode of which a fragment is preserved: "Violet-weaving, pure, sweet-smiling Sappho, I wish to say somewhat, but shame hinders me." And Sappho answered, primly enough, in another ode: "Hadst thou desire of aught good or fair, shame would not have touched thine eyes, but thou wouldst have spoken openly thereof."

The famous story of Sappho's vain pursuit of Phaon, and her death by leaping into the sea from the Leucadian promontory, were, it may safely be stated, inventions of the comic poets. Charles G. D. Roberts, in his introduction to Bliss Carman's exquisite reconstruction of Sappho's lyrics, suggests that the Phaon story is perhaps merely an echo of the legend of Aphrodite and Adonis—who is, indeed, called Phaon in some versions.

But the modern admirers of Sappho have not hesitated to accept as authentic such stories as that of her love for the mythical Phaon, in spite of the fact that they originated 200 years after her death. The Phaon myth, however, Sappho herself might forgive, because of the literature it has begotten— Ovid's immortal epistle and Addison's fantasy, to mention only two examples. But it is too doubtful whether she would appreciate the eloquent but somewhat perfervid hysterical dithyrambs of the late Algernon Charles Swinburne and his followers. The "pure sweet-smiling" poet who scolded her naughty brother and snubbed the ardent Alceus was not:

Love's priestess, mad with pain and joy of song,
Song's priestess, mad with joy and pain of love.

But she was a great poet. If it was not already known, the splendid strophes recovered at Oxyrhyncus would prove it. E. B. Osborn, writing in the London *Morning Post,* has called attention to their resemblance to the Canticle of Canticles, to the way in which, as he says, Love makes Lesbos and land-locked Sharon provinces in one principality. There is a close kinship between the ideas expressed in the first and third stanzas of Sappho's poem and those of these lines:

"I have compared thee, O my love, to a company of horses in Pharaoh's chariots. (I., 9.)

Who is she that looketh forth as the morning, fair as the moon, clear as the sun, and terrible as an army with banners?" (V., 10.)

Lesbos is on the sea, so the picture of the white-winged ships came naturally to the mind of Sappho. But the poet of Sharon thought only of Pharaoh's shining cavalry and of (magic phrase!) an "army with banners."

The world cannot be too grateful to Messrs. Grenfell and Hunt for their literary mining, and to Mr. Edmonds for his marvelously ingenious

[178]

work of reconstruction. We may object to scholars and commentators, we may regret their interpretations, but in this instance men of this sometimes irritating class have made the world's literature their debtor. They have recovered, they have almost recreated, one of the greatest poems of the greatest poet of the greatest age of lyric poetry. It is already a classic, this little song, whose liquid Greek syllables echo the music of undying passion. It is a poem not unworthy of her whom the amazed world called "the miracle"; of whom in our own time that true poet and wise critic, the late Theodore Watts-Dunton, wrote:

Never before these songs were sung, and never since did the human soul, in the grip of a fiery passion, utter a cry like hers, and, from the executive point of view, in directness, in lucidity, in that high, imperious verbal economy which only nature can teach the artist, she has no equal, and none worthy to take the place of second.

THE POETRY OF GERARD HOPKINS

THAT Gerard Hopkins is to-day little known, even among rhymers, is an inevitable result of his manner of life and work. He was a priest of the Catholic Church and a member of the Society of Jesus. His faith was the source of his poetry, but his arduous labors in its service left him little time for celebrating it in verse, and made him so indifferent to applause that he never published. Sir Arthur Quiller-Couch put his "The Starlight Night" in the "Oxford Book of Victorian Verse," and he is represented in Orby Shipley's "Carmina Mariana" and H. C. Beeching's "Lyra Sacra." Several of his poems are included in Volume VIII of "Poets and Poetry of the Century" with a critique by his friend Robert Bridges, and Miss Katherine Brégy has made him the subject of an illuminative essay in her admirable book "The Poet's Chantry." A scant bibliography indeed for a genuinely inspired poet, the most scrupulous wordartist of the nineteenth century!

POETRY OF GERARD HOPKINS

The world is charged with the grandeur of God.
It will flame out like shining from shook foil.

These opening lines of a sonnet illustrate clearly
Gerard Hopkins' spirit and method. Like that
other Jesuit, Robert Southwell, he was a Catholic
poet: for him to write a poem on a secular theme
was difficult, almost impossible. He sang "the
grandeur of God," and for his song he used a
language which in its curious perfection is exclusively his own.

One may search his writings in vain for a figure
that is not novel and true. He took from his own
experience those comparisons that are the material
of poetry, and rejected, it seems, such of them as
already bore marks of use. For him, the grandeur
of God flames out from the world not like light
from stars, but like "shining from shook foil." He
writes not of soft hands, nor of velvety hands, but
of "feel-of-primrose hands." He writes not that
thrush's eggs are blue as the sky, but that they
"look little low heavens." The starry skies of a
winter night are "the dim woods quick with diamond wells," or "the gray lawns cold where quak-
ing gold-dew lies." In Spring "the blue is all in a
rush with richness," and Summer "plashes amid
the billowy apple-trees his lusty hands."

Now, it may be that these exquisite figures would not entitle their maker to high praise if they were isolated bits of splendor, if (like the economical verse-makers of our own day) he had made each one the excuse for a poem. But they come in bewildering profusion. Gerard Hopkins' poems are successions of lovely images, each a poem in itself.

This statement may give its reader the idea that of Gerard Hopkins' poetry may be said, as Charles Ricketts said of Charles Conder's pictures, "There are too many roses." No one who reads his poems, however, will make this criticism. The roses are there of right—all of them. They are, it may be said, necessary roses. They are the cunningly placed elements of an elaborate pattern, a pattern of which roses are the appropriate material. And the red and white of their petals come from the blood and tears that nourished their roots.

It is the overwhelming greatness of this theme that justifies the lavishness of his method. The word "mystic" is nowadays applied so wantonly to every gossiper about things supernatural that it is to most people meaningless. For the benefit of those who know the difference between Saint Theresa and Miss Evelyn Underhill, however, it may be stated that Gerard Hopkins was more nearly a true mystic than either Francis Thompson or Lionel Johnson. The desire, at any rate, for the mystical union with God is evident in every line he wrote, and even more than his friend Coventry Patmore he knew the "dark night of the soul."

This being the case, his theme being God and his writing being an act of adoration, it is profitless to criticize him, as Mr. Robert Bridges has done, for "sacrificing simplicity" and violating those mysterious things, the "canons of taste." A sane editor of a popular magazine would reject everything he wrote. A verse-writer who does not know that "The Habit of Perfection" is true poetry is not a poet. Here it is:

> Elected Silence, sing to me
>   And beat upon my whorlèd ear;
> Pipe me to pastures still, and be
>   The music that I care to hear.
>
> Shape nothing, lips; be lovely-dumb:
>   It is the shut, the curfew sent
> From there where all surrenders come
>   Which only makes you eloquent.
>
> Be shellèd, eyes, with double dark,
>   And find the uncreated light:
> This ruck and reel which you remark
>   Coils, keeps, and teases simple sight.

FUGITIVE PIECES

Palate, the hutch of tasty lust,
  Desire not to be rinsed with wine:
The can must be so sweet, the crust
  So fresh that come in fasts divine!

Nostrils, your careless breath that spend
  Upon the stir and keep of pride,
What relish shall the censers send
  Along the sanctuary side!

O feel-of-primrose hands, O feet
  That want the yield of plushy sward,
But you shall walk the golden street,
  And you unhouse and house the Lord.

And, Poverty, be thou the bride
  And now the marriage feast begun,
And lily-colored clothes provide
  Your spouse, not labored-at, nor spun.

Walter Pater, Gerard Hopkins' tutor at Balliol, had no keener sensitivity to the color and music of language. Gerard Hopkins' purpose—a purpose impossible of fulfillment but not therefore less worth the effort—was "to arrange words like so many separate gems to compose a whole expression of thought, in which the force of grammar and the beauty of rhythm absolutely correspond."

There will always be those who dislike the wealth

of imagery which characterizes Gerard Hopkins' poetry, because they do not understand his mental and spiritual attitude. Perhaps for some critics an altar cloth may be too richly embroidered and a chalice too golden. Ointment of spikenard is "very costly."

PHILOSOPHICAL TENDENCIES IN ENGLISH LITERATURE

WHY do people write poems, stories and plays? The obvious and cynical answer is that people write because they are paid for their writing; the poet makes a poem for the same reason that the carpenter makes a bench, and the dramatist has no motive other than that of the bootmaker. There is some truth in this; if people do not begin to write because they consider writing a means of livelihood they often continue to write for that reason. Certainly it is easy to think of contemporary authors of whom it may safely be said that they have no inspiration save the desire for money.

But the existence of literature is not thus easily to be explained. There are so many trades and professions easier and more profitable than that of letters that he would be a very stupid person indeed who selected it with nothing to influence him in that direction but the desire to make money. There is something else beside the perfectly legitimate desire to make a livelihood in the mind of the writer; there is something that makes him undergo poverty and other tribulations for the sake of his craft.

What is this influence? What is it that makes writers write? It is no one thing. The will to write is related to nearly all the passions, ambitions and desires of mankind; it is the result of instincts immemorial and unchanging. There are those who hold a peculiar inspirational theory about writing, who believe that an author is merely the instrument used by some creative power. In so far as this theory coincides with the truth that God is the source of all energy it is, of course, sound. But those who hold it generally base it on some fantastic idea of genius as a magic, unknowable power, irresponsibly wandering through the world and selecting at random the men and women who are to be through its mysterious spell creative artists. It is a fascinating theory, but untrue, being supported only by the citation of numerous particular cases, which cannot in logic establish a general rule.

A careful examination of the nature of genius would here be out of place. It is sufficient for our purposes to consider genius as extraordinary talent, and to know that it is by no means the inevitable companion of the will to write. The great majority of writers, those who are without skill and those who produce some interesting and even important work, are without genius. Yet they have the will to write. And there have been instances of men and women of undoubted genius so lazy that they seemed absolutely to lack the creative urge present in the minds of their less gifted brothers and sisters.

There would be writers if there were no such thing as genius just as there would be writers if it were impossible to make money by writing. Consider the earliest days when first by means of crude symbols chiseled on a rock or by means of rough combinations of sounds a man endeavored to convey to his fellows some message not necessitated by the ordinary conditions of life—some message important for its own sake alone. What caused this man to carve, to chant, to express ideas so that they would be intelligible to his fellows? If we understand the motives for this man's conduct, if we find out what made him a creative artist, we shall understand why modern man writes. For the motives, emotions, essential habits of mankind do not greatly change with the passing of the ages; the soul of man has the changelessness of immortal things.

Motives are hard to trace and they are usually

found in combination. We cannot be sure that the first writer had only one motive, but we can imagine many motives, any one of which would have been sufficient to cause his literary adventure. These may be indicated as the urge to chronicle, the urge to attract, the urge to worship, and the urge to create. And all these are related to and possibly included by the need of self-expression.

Among the simplest and least literary people, events that greatly disturb the routine of life—wars, famines, pestilences, earthquakes—seem to develop writers automatically. The great thing has happened and must have a record safer than man's fickle memory. So inevitably come the chronicler and his chronicle. The demand creates the supply. But the desire to ensure remembrance of events is not in itself sufficient to ensure the existence of literature. There is also what I have termed the urge to attract. The savage warrior may carve on stone or paint upon a strip of pale bark a record of his own brave victory or ingenious escape. This he does to attract the attention and admiration of his public, such as it is, to his courage and intelligence. And also the mere making of the record is in itself an achievement certain to bring to its maker the wonder and esteem of those lacking this strange power. And this sort of admiration, he finds, comes to him even when the things about which he writes are not his own doings. So subjective art comes into existence. Man writes because of the urge to worship to-day, as he has always done. He utters prayers that have been provided for his needs by divinely constituted authorities, and to the unspoken ejaculation of his heart he silently gives the best literary form possible to him—the directness and passionate simplicity proper to great literature. He repeats, when he prays in accordance with the forms prescribed by the Church, great literature which came into existence originally in response to the urge to worship. And in all languages the writings of most enduring loveliness, even apart from those divinely inspired, are those which relate most closely to worship—those writings made immortal by the love of God. So writers may fulfill the purpose for which they are made by writing—may know God better by writing about Him, increase their love of Him by expressing it in beautiful words, serve Him in this world by means of their best talent, and because of this service and His mercy be happy with Him forever in Heaven.

There is also the motive which perhaps gives

rise to the common and fallacious idea of the writer's inspiration—the motive which I have designated as the urge to create. Of course the only true creator is God, and for a creature to seem to create may be a perilous thing, savoring of blasphemy. Certainly the evil egotism of some writers, using their talent for the destruction of their souls and those of others, is a blasphemous thing. This is a matter better suited for discussion by a moral theologian than by a critic, but surely it is possible for the writer to assay his task of creating a work of art the more humbly and the more joyfully because it is done in reverent imitation of the Maker or Poet of the universe.

Now, a writer does not analyze or separate his motives. They all are related to and possibly included by the need of self-expression. There is an idea in the writer's brain which he wishes to put into words and on paper. He does so, without bothering to try to discover why he has this impulse.

The existence of these motives, in various combinations, is evident in all literature. The novelist wishes to create a thing of beauty, to chronicle certain actual or possible events, to attract admiration to himself and perhaps to a certain class or race of men. If he is a great writer he has also, even if he be not thoroughly conscious of it, the desire to worship—he uses his talent honestly and skillfully, for God's sake, making an acceptable offering. He may write a drama of modern life, a story of pioneer days in the Far West, a sonnet to a buttercup, a pamphlet in favor of improved tenement houses, a history of the Spanish-American War. Whatever he may write, his desire is to chronicle, at attract, and to create. And if he be a great writer his desire also is to worship.

The power and desire to influence thought possessed by skillful writers has caused the world sometimes to regard them as actually the leaders of mankind's spiritual and intellectual endeavors. Writers themselves are quick to take this point of view; we have in America hundreds of popular novelists who have no hesitation in advising humanity about all its moral problems, thousands of minor poets who will answer the questions of the ages in a sonnet or a handful of free verse. There are some reasons for the writers to be justly considered leaders of popular thought. As a class, they understand humanity, and sympathize with it. They have the passions and hopes and loves of the rest of the world, intensified. Also they have a sense of artistic, or, as it is called, poetic justice, and poetic justice usually is Christian justice.

But writers are unfitted to be leaders of popular thought by many disqualifications inseparable from their craft. Interested as they are in the rest of humanity, they inevitably are set apart from it by reason of their exceptional gift. They show their sense of this separation, even when they do not openly admit it, by dressing and talking and living in a manner different from that common to their fellow-citizens. The velvet jacket, the long hair, the flowing necktie, the Bohemian studio, the defiance of custom and sometimes of law—these things are indications of that separation from mankind which makes the writer an unsafe leader of popular thought. There is also the danger that the writer will, if he become a leader of thought, grow intoxicated with power, and lead thought irresponsibly, foolishly, wickedly, having in mind not the welfare of humanity but the delight of leadership. To this temptation all leaders of thought—politicians, educators, investigators—are liable, but the writers most of all.

The proper function of the writer is rather to interpret than to lead the thought of his time. Seldom does a writer actually give the world a new idea. What he does is to give expression to an idea which has lain dormant in the mind of the people awaiting his revealing and quickening touch. There is a hope or a fear in the minds of men—it finds expression in deeds and simultaneously in words. The events in a nation's history and the intellectual and spiritual causes of those events are revealed to later generations by the poets and storytellers. The historical development of nations is clear to the students of the world's literature. Take the American Civil War for an example—we find the soul of the North revealed in "Marching Through Georgia" and the "Battle Hymn of the Republic" and the soul of the South in "Dixie" and in "Maryland, My Maryland." No volumes of history give us a clearer understanding of the feelings of our fathers than do these poems. So also I believe that the awakening to a sense of the evil of the so-called Reformation, that awakening which is historically recorded by the events associated with the Oxford Movement, found literary expression in the poetry of Rossetti and Patmore and the other members of the Pre-Raphaelite Brotherhood.

Since the development which history records is merely the outward and visible sign of an inward and spiritual progress, therefore the proper themes of creative literary artists are those things which the professed historians cannot treat—the hidden things, the essentials of history. So the writers whose work endures are those who concern themselves with the interior, not the exterior, of life. The great writers are the spiritual historians of their generation. Physical man is important only in relation to spiritual man. Man by himself, man not considered in respect to God, is unworthy of the attention of any writer. The men and women whose plays and poems and stories endure are those who see that one cannot "know himself" if he "presume not God to scan." They know that the proper study of mankind, and the theme of all literature worthy of the name, is the soul of man.

Literature is a matter of spiritual chronicle and interpretation. Therefore its beauty must, as Keats said, be truth. The writer approaches beauty in proportion as the subject of his interpretation approaches truth. It is a fact that a writer may express an idea which seems contrary to the feeling of his time—may praise economic justice, for instance, in the day of great industrial tyranny, or in general express idealism among materialists. But this should not make us consider him an untruthful interpreter. Ideas implicit in the people may be explicit in the writer. And again the writer may express the thought of a minority more significant than the majority.

The popularity of a writer may be geographical or temporal—perhaps numerical would give a clearer idea of my meaning than geographical. That is, he may be read in his own time by many people, spread over a great part of the world's surface, or he may have the attention of a public which is great because it extends through the ages. The second sort of popularity is that which the great writers receive, and sometimes they have the first kind also. The great writer, the universal writer, is universal in his theme. And there is only one theme that is universal—God.

TWO LECTURES ON ENGLISH POETRY

THE BALLAD

I BEGIN the consideration of the forms of versification with the ballad, for two reasons. In the first place, this is historically the correct procedure. The earliest English poetry that has come down to us is in this form; it is the ballad that, recited in the great hall of the castle on a Winter evening by some wandering bard, delighted the simple hearts of our remote forefathers, strong, rude men, few of whom ever tasted the dainties that are bred in a book. The ballad gave pleasure not only to the lord and his lady, as they reclined in their great oaken chairs, but also the chaplain and the men-at-arms and the serving folk clustered together toward the foot of the table. For the ballad is universal in its appeal, it is the most democratic kind of poetry. Perhaps it is not the most primitive sort; the songs of worship or praise or love which grew out of the earliest dance rituals may have been more closely akin to the lyric. But these songs must soon have developed into a recital of the deeds of the god or hero celebrated; they must have taken on that narrative style which is the essential of the ballad. We may choose to call Chaucer's "Canterbury Pilgrims" an epic, if we will, but even so we cannot avoid the feeling that it is a sequence of ballads. And after all an epic is nothing but a ballad de luxe.

The second reason for considering the ballad first among the forms of English verse is the ease with which it may be written. It is the simplest form of poetical composition, and the novice in the craft of versification will not find it difficult to attain in it, after a few attempts, a fair measure of success.

What is the ballad? Let me begin by saying what it is not. It is not a brief song, although of late years the word has been generally used to designate almost any rimed composition set to music. People who speak of some of the popular songs of the day as "sentimental ballads" are using the term incorrectly. They mean, as a rule, "sentimental lyrics." In bygone years the ballad was sung, or at any rate recited, to the accompaniment of a harp or other stringed instrument. But in modern times the lyric is almost the only sort of poetry to receive a musical setting.

Furthermore, the ballad is not the ballade. The ballade is a highly artificial form of verse, French in origin, consisting, as a rule, of three eight-line stanzas and a four-line envoi, with only three rhymes in all twenty-eight lines. People with a taste for untra-modern spelling sometimes label these productions "ballads" instead of "ballades," and other people sometimes try to give their ballads an archaic flavor by labeling them "ballades." Both practices are utterly unjustifiable. A ballade is no more a ballad than a sonnet is a quatrain.

What, then, is a ballad? In "On the History of the Ballads, 1100-1500" (Proceedings of the British Academy, Volume IV), Professor W. P. Ker writes: "The truth is that the ballad is an ideal, a poetical form, which can take up any matter, and does not leave that matter as it was before." But this, of course, is no definition. It would apply equally well to all forms of poetry. Professor Ker continues: "In spite of Socrates and his logic we may venture to say, in answer to the question 'What is a ballad?'—'A Ballad is "The Milldams of Binnorie" and "Sir Patrick Spens" and "The Douglas Tragedy" and "Lord Randal" and "Childe Maurice," and things of that sort.' "

That greatest of anthologists, Sir Arthur Quiller-Couch, quotes these remarks of Professor Ker in the preface to his volume "The Oxford Book of Ballads," a book which every lover of poetry and especially every member of the craft of verse-making should possess. He goes on to supplement Professor Ker's definition, or rather description, by quoting lines from a number of famous ballads of ancient days, and saying that the ballad is these things also and in proof of the statement that ballads are diverse in manner and theme he mentions as latter-day ballad-makers poets having so little in common as Sir Walter Scott, Coleridge and Rudyard Kipling. Thus do Professor Ker and Sir Arthur Quiller-Couch evade the task of definition-making. But they are critics of poetry and therefore entitled to the use of escapes and evasions denied to the author of a text-book. Let me therefore say with no thought of originality in the saying, that a ballad is a story told in verse. Usually it is told in a sequence of quatrains, with one rhyme to a stanza, and usually the line is the iambic heptameter—or rather the stanza consists of two iambic tetrameters and two iambic trimeters. But this form is not inevitable; the only thing inevitable about a ballad is that it shall be a story.

Of the ancient ballads there are many collections,

of which the most famous are those of Bishop Percy and of Professor Child. But Sir Arthur Quiller-Couch's book, already mentioned, is sufficiently comprehensive for the needs of the ordinary student of the subject.

In the preface to this book, Sir Arthur says a rather surprising thing. He says: "While the lyric in general, still making for variety, is to-day more prolific than ever and (all cant apart) promises fruit to equal the best, that particular offshoot which we call the ballad has been dead, or as good as dead, for two hundred years."

It is hard to understand why Sir Arthur Quiller-Couch made this statement. In his "The Oxford Book of English Verse" and "The Oxford Book of Victorian Verse" he had included so many true ballads—Rossetti's "The Blessed Damozel," and Dobell's "Keith of Ravelston"—which is as authentic a ballad as "Thomas the Rhymer" or "Sir Patrick Spens." Also Kipling was making genuine ballads of land and water, and Henry Newbolt was writing his glorious ballads of the British Navy. The ballad was far from dead; it was no longer the only popular form of poetry, but it had not ceased to thrive. And the Great War seems to have given English and American poets new enthusiasm for this form so suited to the chronicling of deeds of valor.

I have said that the true ballad was a story told in verse. Let me add that, according to the strictest interpretation of the term, the story must be told throughout in the third person—the narrator must be merely a narrator, he cannot figure in the tale. This is true of most of the old ballads. There are exceptions to the rule, however, notably "Archie of Cawfield" and the immortal "Helen of Kirconnel." Nor is it necessary that the modern ballad-maker should take pains to eliminate his own personality from his work, the modern tendency seems to be toward subjectivity in poetry and the verse-maker who seeks popular approval will be guided by popular tastes.

It is true that the very greatest of the ballads are those which were written in the days when the ballad had not to compete with other forms. But in accordance with the principle underlying this work—that of exhibiting the work of successful modern poetic craftsmen, I will not quote "Sir Patrick Spens" or "Hugh of Lincoln" or "Cospatrick" or "Little Musgrave and Lady Barnard" or any other classic. Instead, I will call the reader's attention to the work of some of the poets who, in our own time, have been proving the falsity of Sir Arthur Quiller-Couch's statement.

THE SONNET

I said that the ballad was the most primitive form of English verse composition of which examples have come down to us, and that it was the easiest form to write. I now come to what might almost be called the antithesis of the ballad—the sonnet. The ballad is simple, the sonnet is complex; the ballad appeals to the uneducated, being, as I said, merely a short story in verse, while the sonnet appeals chiefly to those who have a cultivated taste for poetry. It is easy, I said, to write a passable ballad; to write a sonnet that is merely correct in technique is a difficult matter, and to write a good sonnet calls for the exercise of all a verse-maker's patience, ingenuity and talent.

Theodore Watts-Dunton, himself an accomplished sonneteer, finds the sonnet as "in the literature of modern Europe, a brief poetic form of fourteen rhymed verses, ranged according to prescription." This definition is open to criticism in two respects. In the first place it is redundant, since a poem of fourteen lines necessarily is brief. In the second place Watts-Dunton neglected to

state that the length of the line is arbitrarily fixed—
if the lines are not iambic pentameters, the poem is
not a sonnet.

The first requirements of the sonnet, then, are
that it shall have fourteen lines, and that these
lines shall be iambic pentameters. Furthermore,
the rhyme scheme is arbitrarily fixed, and the number of rhymes arbitrarily limited in such a way as
to add greatly to the verse-maker's labor.

The simplest form of the sonnet is what is called
the Shakespearean sonnet, from its use in the
famous sequence in which the greatest of English
poets is said to have "unlocked his heart"—although this does not seem a fair description of it,
when we consider the great library of books in
which attempts are made to explain what Shakespeare meant in these sonnets. This form consists
merely of the quatrains, rhyming *a, b, a, b, c, d, c,
d, e, f, e, f,* followed by a rhymed couplet. The
lines are, as in all forms of the sonnet, iambic
pentameters.

Obviously, this form presents no real difficulty
to the verse-maker with a fair degree of talent. Its
use by Shakespeare gives it a certain authority, and
some critics, notably Professor Israel Gollancz, of
London University, say that it is better suited the

English language than the more usual or Petrarchan form. Nevertheless, the weight of opinion is against this form. Many critics deny that three quatrains followed by a couplet constitute a true sonnet, and Professor Brander Matthews always calls this form not a sonnet but a "fourteener." Modern English poets who have written Shakespearean sonnets are few in number. George Eliot wrote a sequence in this form, but did not thereby add to her fame. In fact, the only notable use of the Shakespearean sonnet form during the last half century is to be found in John Masefield's "Good Friday and Other Poems," which contain a sequence of introspective and philosophical Shakespearean sonnets, so lofty in thought and appropriate in expression as actually to suggest the work of the poet who first greatly made use of their instrument.

The form generally used by poets writing in English is what is called the Petrarchan sonnet. In its simplest but not its easiest form, this consists of a division of eight lines called the octave and a division of six lines called the sestet, the rhyme scheme of the octave being *a, b, b, a, a, b, b, a,* and that of the sestet being *c, d, c, d, c, d.* Here we have, you see, only four rhymes in all the fourteen lines. An excellent example of the Petrarchan sonnet of this exact type is Austin Dobson's "Don Quixote."

DON QUIXOTE

BY AUSTIN DOBSON

Behind thy pasteboard, on thy battered hack,
  Thy lean cheek striped with plaster to and fro,
  Thy long spear levelled at the unseen foe,
And doubtful Sancho trudging at thy back,
Thou wert a figure strange enough, good lack!
  To make wiseacredom, both high and low,
    Rub purblind eyes, and (having watched thee
      go)
Dispatch its Dogberrys upon thy track:

Alas! poor Knight! Alas! poor soul possest!
  Yet would to-day, when Courtesy grows chill,
And life's fine loyalties are turned to jest,
  Some fire of thine might burn within us still!
Ah, would but one might lay his lance in rest
  And charge in earnest—were it but a mill!

This is a good sonnet to study for several reasons. In the first place the accuracy of the form makes it an excellent model. And in the second place it illustrates what I have to say as to the correspondence in the thought of the sonnet and its form.

Now, there have been attempts to make a sonnet the vehicle of a narrative; these attempts have seldom been successful. A sonnet is descriptive and interpretative in theme, and it must give at the very least two aspects of interpretations of the emotion, idea, or object with which it deals. One of these must be in the octave and the other in the sestet. Sometimes the idea is merely expressed or described in the octave, and explained in the sestet, sometimes the idea in the octave suggests a different idea in the sestet—the point to remember is that there must be a change in the thought marked by the beginning of the sonnet's ninth line.

This we see admirably illustrated in Austin Dobson's "Don Quixote." In the first four lines we have a graphic picture of the mad knight of La Mancha, and a statement of the effect this vision has upon those who are wise in this world. But the very first words of the sestet show the development in the thought. The poet ceases to describe, instead he expresses emotion, he expresses his pity, his sympathy, his admiration for Don Quixote, and his wish that the knight might find a successor in our own day. The octave has its climax and the sestet has its climax, and the two sections of the poem are related by the continuity of thought, and divided by the contrast of ideas.

This type of sonnet was called by Watts-Dunton the sonnet of flow and ebb—the significance of this term being that the thought flowed to the end of the octave and ebbed from that point to the close of the sestet. Commenting on this John Addington Symonds wrote: "The striking metaphorical symbol drawn from the observation of the swelling and declining wave can even in some examples be applied to sonnets on the Shakespearean model; for, as a wave may fall gradually or abruptly, so the sonnet may sink with stately volume or with precipitate subsidence to its close."

For a verse-maker to give his sonnet this requisite flow and ebb of idea, and keep at the same time his rhyme scheme accurate is no easy matter. And the very difficulty of the form is a strong argument in favor of its frequent use by novices in versification. If you can write a sonnet that is technically correct, you need fear none of the difficulties that any other kind of verse-making will present. The accuracy and condensation, the concentration of thought, the straight-forwardness of statement, which are the distinguishing marks of the well-turned sonnet are the most valuable tools which a verse writer can have. In writing, as well as he can, one sonnet, the verse-maker will learn more than he could learn in writing half a dozen ballads or twenty volumes full of unrhymed free verse.

This book is intended for the guidance not of poets but of verse-makers. Yet I cannot forbear quoting Watts-Dunton's admirable statement of the whole content of the sonnet. He writes: "Without being wholly artificial, like the rondeau, the sestina, the ballade, the villanelle, and the rest, the sonnet is yet so artistic in structure, its form is so universally known, recognized, and adopted as being artistic, that the too fervid spontaneity and reality of the poet's emotion may be in a certain degree veiled, and the poet can whisper, as from behind a mask, those deepest secrets of the heart which could otherwise only find expression in purely dramatic forms."

As I said, the simplest, and in some respects, the most difficult form of sonnet, has for the rhyme scheme $a, b, b, a, a, b, b, a, c, d, c, d, c, d$. But there is a tendency to vary the rhyme scheme in the sestet —the octave usually is unchanged. One common variation is to have the rhymes of the sestet $c, d, e, c, d, e,$ instead of c, d, c, d, c, d. This is the scheme

we find followed in the sestet of two of "Three Sonnets on Oblivion," by a distinguished American
poet, Mr. George Sterling.

THREE SONNETS OF OBLIVION

BY GEORGE STERLING

Oblivion

Her eyes have seen the monoliths of kings
    Upcast like foam of the effacing tide;
    She hath beheld the desert stars deride
The monuments of power's imaginings:
About their base the wind Assyrian flings
    The dust that throned the satrap in his pride;
    Cambyses and the Memphian pomps abide
As in the flame the moth's presumptuous wings.

There gleams no glory that her hand shall spare,
    Nor any sun whose days shall cross her night,
Whose realm enfolds man's empire and its end.
    No armour of renown her sword shall dare,
    No council of the gods withstand her might—
    Stricken at last Time's lonely Titans bend.

The Night of Gods

Their mouths have drunken the eternal wine—
    The draught that Baal in oblivion sips.
    Unseen about their courts the adder slips,
Unheard the sucklings of the leopard whine;

The toad has found a resting-place divine,
    And bloats in stupor between Ammon's lips.
    O Carthage and the unreturning ships,
The fallen pinnacle, the shifting Sign!

Lo! when I hear from voiceless court and fane
    Time's adoration of eternity,—
        The cry of kingdoms past and gods undone,—
I stand as one whose feet at noontide gain
    A lonely shore; who feels his soul set free,
        And hears the blind sea chanting to the sun.

In these two sonnets, you see, Mr. Sterling has in his sestet the rhymes *c, d, e, c, d, e,* thus having more license than the poet of the sonnet in four rhymes. He uses the same number of rhymes in the final sonnet of this trilogy, but varies the order of the rhymes in the sestet, having for his scheme not *c, d, e, c, d, e,* but *c, d, d, e, c, e.* One objection to this method is that it produces, as you see, a rhymed couplet in the midst of the sestet.

The Dust Dethroned

Sargon is dust, Semiramis a clod.
    In crypts profaned the moon at midnight peers;
    The owl upon the Sphinx hoots in her ears,
And scant and dere the desert grasses nod
Where once the armies of Assyria trod,
    With younger sunlight splendid on the spears;

The lichens cling the closer with the years,
And seal the eyelids of the weary god.

Where high the tombs of royal Egypt heave,
  The vulture shadows with arrested wings
  The indecipherable boasts of kings,
    Till Arab children hear their mother's cry
And leave in mockery their toy—they leave
    The skull of Pharaoh staring at the sky.

It is seldom that we find such a couplet as: "The vulture shadows with arrested wings, The indecipherable boasts of kings," in the midst of the sestet. But there are many verse writers who use the couplet, unrelated in rhyme to the rest of the sestet, to conclude the sonnet. This of course was Shakespeare's method, but Shakespeare, as we have seen, was not making Petrarchan sonnets. The great danger is that the final couplet will give the conclusion of the sonnet too much of a snap, too much of an epigrammatic flavor. Therefore it is well to avoid this device, although it cannot be denied that some of the greatest sonnets in the language end in a couplet. Some years ago I asked a number of English and American poets and critics to name their favorite brief poems. Many of them chose sonnets, and one of them, Mr. Edward J. Wheeler, a critic of experience and discrimination, for many years the President of the Poetry Society of America, selected a sonnet ending in a couplet—Blanco White's "Night." It may be remarked that this famous sonnet is almost the only one of Blanco White's many compositions to escape oblivion.

NIGHT

BY JOSEPH BLANCO WHITE

Mysterious Night! when our first parent knew
  Thee from report divine, and heard thy name,
  Did he not tremble for this lovely frame,
This glorious canopy of light and blue?
Yet 'neath a curtain of translucent dew,
  Bathed in the rays of the great setting flame,
  Hesperus with the host of heaven came,
And lo! creation widened in man's view.

Who could have thought such darkness lay con-
  cealed
  Within thy beams, O Sun! or who could find,
Whilst fly and leaf and insect stood revealed,
  That to such countless orbs thou mad'st us blind!
Why do we then shun Death with anxious strife?
If Light can thus deceive, wherefore not Life?

Here is another sonnet ending in a couplet, which I quote for several reasons. In the first place, the poet, while using the couplet, has avoided the dangers of the epigram. In the second place, he comes as close to writing a narrative as the sonneteer may safely do. In the third place he deviates from the strict rules of the sonnet in one important particular, which should be at once apparent to every student of the subject. I do not refer to the false rhyme of "Africa" and "bar"—the deviation which I mean refers only to the sonnet form, and has to do with the arrangement of the thought.

BOOKRA

BY CHARLES DUDLEY WARNER

One night I lay asleep in Africa,
　In a closed garden by the city gate;
　A desert horseman, furious and late,
Came wildly thundering at the massive bar,
"Open in Allah's name! Wake, Mustapha!
Slain is the Sultan,—treason, war, and hate
　Rage from Fez to Tetuan! Open straight."
The watchman heard as thunder from afar:

"Go to! in peace this city lies asleep;
　To all-knowing Allah 'tis no news you bring";
Then turned in slumber still his watch to keep.
　At once a nightingale began to sing,
In oriental calm the garden lay,—
Panic and war postponed another day.

LECTURES ON ENGLISH POETRY

The deviation to which I refer is the lack of absolute distinction between the octave and the sestet. If the rules of the sonnet were strictly followed, the line which introduces the watchman would begin the sestet instead of closing the octave.

The best form of the Petrarchan sonnet for the novice in versification to use in practice is the form I first described, that in which the rhyme scheme is *a, b, b, a, a, b, b, a, c, d, c, d, c, d.* But if you find that this at first presents insurmountable difficulty, use three rhymes in the sestet instead of two, as in the two poems following. In these, you will see, the rhyme scheme of the sestet is *c, d, e, c, d, e.* The first is a deeply introspective study by one of the greatest women poets of our generation; the second is more true to the traditional type of sonnet in thought, giving the subject in the octave, and the lesson drawn therefrom in the sestet. It is the work of a young American poet whose name is familiar to every reader of American magazines.

RENOUNCEMENT

BY ALICE MEYNELL

I must not think of thee; and, tired yet strong,
  I shun the love that lurks in all delight—
  The love of thee—and in the blue heaven's height,

FUGITIVE PIECES

And in the dearest passage of a song.
Oh, just beyond the fairest thoughts that throng
   This breast, the thought of thee waits hidden yet
       bright;
   But it must never, never come in sight;
I must stop short of thee the whole day long.

But when sleep comes to close each difficult day,
   When night gives pause to the long watch I keep,
     And all my bonds I need must lay apart,
Must doff my will as raiment laid away,—
   With the first dream that comes with the first
     sleep
     I run, I run, I am gathered to thy heart.

CANDLE-LIGHT

BY THOMAS S. JONES, JR.

As in old days of mellow candle-light,
   A little flame of gold beside the pane
   Where icy branches blowing in the rain
Seem spectre fingers of a ghostly night;
Yet on the hearth the fire is warm and bright,
   The homely kettle steams a soft refrain,
   And to one's mind old things rush back again,
Sweet tender things still young in death's despite.

So, when the winter blasts across life's sea
   Do beat about my door and shale the walls
     Until the house must sink upon the sand,

[216]

Then on some magic wind of memory,
  Borne swiftly to my heart a whisper falls,—
    And on my arm the pressure of your hand!

Here is another famous modern sonnet, in which
the three rhymes of the sestet are arranged in the
order *c, d, e, e, c, d.*

THE ODYSSEY

BY ANDREW LANG

As one that for a weary space has lain
  Lulled by the song of Circe and her wine
  In gardens near the pale of Proserpine,
Where that Æaean isle forgets the main,
And only the low lutes of love complain,
  And only shadows of wan lovers pine,—
    As such an one were glad to know the brine
Salt on his lips, and the large air again,—

So gladly, from the songs of modern speech
  Men turn, and see the stars, feel the free
    Shrill wind beyond the close of heavy flowers,
    And through the music of the languid hours,
They hear like ocean on a western beach
  The surge and thunder of the Odyssey.

This sonnet has been criticized by Professor
Brander Matthews, not on account of its rhyme
scheme, but because of its lack of what he calls

tone-color. I will discuss the subject of tone-color later, but it may be well at this point to explain that this criticism means that the rhymes of this sonnet are not sufficiently varied—that "lain" does not differ sufficiently from "wine," and "free" does not differ sufficiently from "beach" (the first two words being similar in consonantal value, and the second two in vowel value) to warrant their use— the theory being that the rhymes used in a sonnet should contrast strongly with each other—"lain" and "hide," for example, and "free" and "shore," for example, contrasting more strikingly than the words used. This contrast in tone-color, to use that phrase, may be noticed in this strongly-wrought sonnet of William Watson's. How strikingly the sound of "old," in the octave contrasts with that of "ing," and how strikingly in the sestet "ove" contrasts with "ire." The poet uses but two rhymes in the sestet, the arrangement being *c, d, d, c, d, c.*

TO ONE WHO HAD WRITTEN IN DERISION OF THE BELIEF IN IMMORTALITY

BY WILLIAM WATSON

Dismiss not so, with light hard phrase and cold,
   Ev'n if it be but fond imagining,
   The hope whereto so passionately cling .

The dreaming generations from of old!
Not thus, to luckless men, are tidings told
   Of mistress lost, or riches taken wing;
   And is eternity a slighter thing,
To have or lose, than kisses or than gold?

Nay, tenderly, if needs thou must, disprove
   My loftiest fancy, dash my grand desire
   To see this curtain lift, these clouds retire,
And Truth, a boundless dayspring, blaze above
   And round me; and to ask of my dead sire
His pardon for a word that wronged his love.

Of course you will find exceptions to the rules I
have stated, you will find poets who have combined
the Shakespearean and Petrarchan sonnet. The
most usual way of doing this is to end the Petrarchan sonnet with the couplet typical of the Shakespearean form, as in Blanco White's "Night." But
sometimes we find the octave of the sonnet consisting, as in the Shakespearean form, of two quatrains,
and the sestet approaching closely to the Petrarchan
idea. Such a sonnet is "Letty's Globe," by Charles
Tennyson-Turner, the brother of Alfred Tennyson.
In this the octave is Shakespearean—rhyming $a, b,$
$a, b, c, d, c, d,$ but the sestet rhymes $e, f, f, g, e, g.$

FUGITIVE PIECES

LETTY'S GLOBE

BY CHARLES TENNYSON-TURNER

When Letty had scarce passed her third glad year,
  And her young, artless words began to flow,
One day we gave the child a coloured sphere
  Of the wide earth, that she might mark and know,
By tint and outline, all its sea and land.
  She patted all the world; old empires peeped
Between her baby fingers; her soft hand
  Was welcome at all frontiers. How she leaped,
And laughed, and prattled in her world-wide bliss;
  But when we turned her sweet unlearned eye
  On our own isle, she raised a joyous cry,
    "Oh! yes, I see it, Letty's home is there!"
And while she hid all England with a kiss,
  Bright over Europe fell her golden hair.

You will find also exceptions to the rule that the thought of the sonnet shall be sharply differentiated by the pause between the octave and the sestet, that it shall flow in the octave and ebb in the sestet. John Milton, for instance, certainly the author of some of the greatest sonnets in the English tongue, blended the octave of his sonnets with their sestets, letting, as a critic has said, "octave flow into sestet without break of music or thought." Thus, says Watts-Dunton, Milton, in his use of the Petrarchan octave and sestet for the embodiment of intellectual substance incapable of that partial disintegration which Petrarch himself always or mostly sought, invented a species of sonnet which is English in impetus, but Italian, or partly Italian, in structure. But these innovations are for the Miltons of our literature, not for the apprentices of the craft. We must know how to write longhand before we can write shorthand; we must know the axioms before we can propound original geometric theories. Until he has demonstrated his ability to write a poem consisting of fourteen iambic pentameters with the rhyme scheme *a, b, b, a, a, b, b, a, c, d, c, d,* the maker of verses should not experiment with any variations of the established form.

GILBERT K. CHESTERTON AND HIS POETRY

GILBERT K. CHESTERTON is an essayist, a novelist, a dramatist, a debater and a poet. But many people—his brother, Cecil Chesterton, did for instance—believe that he is first of all a poet. And certainly it is in his poetry that his characteristic style is most easily recognized and defined.

Mr. Chesterton and the late Henry James are not very often thought of as intellectual or spiritual brothers. And yet there is a startlingly obvious resemblance between these two writers. Both are stylists; both have thoroughly mastered certain peculiar methods of speech, and both are, it must be confessed, hampered by their undeviating loyalty to these methods.

This is not the place to analyze the style of Mr. James. It is sufficient to recall to the reader's mind the fact that the author of "The Golden Bowl" was not concerned so much with the presentation of extraordinary ideas as with the extraordinary presentation of ordinary ideas. And the extraordinariness of his presentation consisted in its thorough-ness; he was not content to suggest the thing or to show one aspect of it; he was able, and seemed to feel a certain moral obligation, to present every aspect of the thing, to give all its dimensions, characteristics, origins and possibilities. His method may roughly be indicated by saying that it is the opposite of impressionism.

Gilbert K. Chesterton's method, which is more readily observed and defined in his poetry than in his prose, also consists chiefly of the extraordinary presentation of ordinary ideas. But he does not attempt to give every aspect and shading of an idea. Rather he attempts to present that aspect of an idea which, while true, is sufficiently unusual to surprise the reader; the theory being that the attention attracted by the unusualness will be held by the truth.

This method is admirably suited to the uses of fiction, as "The Ball and the Cross" and "The Man Who Was Thursday" show. It is effective in debate, and in controversial essays on matters ethical and political, as is shown by the writings of Mr. Chesterton himself and of that school of popular apologetics which he may be said to have founded. In poetry it is sometimes almost magically effective, and sometimes grotesquely inappropriate. The perfect, and most lamentable, example of the use of this method is to be found in a poem called "E. C. B." These initials evidently are those of Chesterton's friend, Edmund Clerihew Bentley, the writer of detective stories.

In this serious and, for the most part, beautiful poem, Mr. Chesterton tells us that because of the virtue of one man he finds something to love in every man. Bentley is a man, he says, therefore, for Bentley's sake no man is to be hated. For the sake of Bentley's humanity, Chesterton says that he loves everyone, the murderer, the hypocrite, even—and this is the great climax—himself.

I should say, this was to be his great climax. But the method seizes him, and keeps him from saying anything so strongly simple as "I love myself." Instead, he says:

> I love the man I saw but now
> Hanging head downwards in the well.

This is, as I said, the Chestertonian method at its worst. Here you find the poet absolutely at the mercy of his method, made to say a simple thing in a complicated manner. But this is, it is only fair to say, an early poem, and not fairly representative of

Chesterton as a poet. For it is pleasant to see that, unlike Henry James, Chesterton has been steadily mastering his style, mastering it so thoroughly that he can lay it aside when it is inappropriate. He lays it aside, for instance, in some of the passionate and most effective chapters of "The Crimes of England." And he lays it aside in such of his writings as best deserve the name of poetry.

Like every poet however original, Chesterton has "played the sedulous ape to many masters." In his stirring ballads of warfare, such as "The Battle of Gibson" and "Lepanto" I find echoes of the last of the great ballad makers, Macaulay, whom Francis Thompson himself did not disdain to imitate. In his political controversial poems I find strong suggestions of a poet whose point of view Chesterton is far from sharing—Rudyard Kipling. I find also a curious suggestion of Elizabeth Barrett Browning. Mrs. Browning was Evangelical where Chesterton is Catholic in thought, and she had a fatal knack of taking the wrong point of view in political matters—Italian affairs, for example. But she was genuinely a democrat and genuinely religious, and it is strange to see how often she and Chesterton think alike. There is even a similarity of phraseology, as when Chesterton writes:

FUGITIVE PIECES

The Christ Child lay on Mary's lap.
    His hair was like a crown.
And all the flowers looked up to Him,
    And all the stars looked down.

whereas many years before Elizabeth Barrett Browning in her poem "The Doves" had written of a palm tree:

The tropic flowers looked up to it,
    The tropic stars looked down.

Walt Whitman and Gilbert K. Chesterton seem a strange combination. But Chesterton himself has acknowledged that he found in "Leaves of Grass" a great and wholesome inspiration. This seems strange to us, for the American Whitmanite or Whitmaniac is a pale long-haired creature of many 'isms, directly the opposite of a robust Christian like Chesterton. But in the eighteen-nineties when "science announced nonentity and art admired decay" Walt Whitman's "barbaric yawp sounding over the roofs of the world" seemed a healthy sound. So in his dedication to "The Man Who Was Thursday," Chesterton writes:

Not all unhelped we held the fort, our tiny flags
    unfurled;

Some giants laboured in that crowd to lift it from
the world.
I find again the book we found, I feel the hour that
flings
Far out of fish-shaped Paumanok some cry of
cleaner things;
And the Green Carnation withered, as in forest
fires that pass,
Roared in the wind of all the world ten million
leaves of grass;
Or sane and sweet and sudden as a bird sings in
the rain—
Truth out of Tusitala spoke and pleasure out of
pain.
Yea, cool and clear and sudden as a bird sings in
the grey,
Dunedin to Samoa spoke, and darkness unto day.
But we were young; we lived to see God break the
bitter charms,
God and the good Republic come riding back in
arms:
We have seen the city of Mansoul, even as it rocked,
relieved—
Blessed are they who did not see, but being blind,
believed.

For some reason, it is difficult to think of Chesterton in love. We can readily think of him fighting or praying, but to think of him making love re-

quires an effort of the imagination. Yet he is happily married, and while his love poems are few, they are noble in thought and beautiful in expression. One of the most personal and characteristic of them is that to which he gives the name "Confessional."

CONFESSIONAL

Now that I kneel at the throne, O Queen,
Pity and pardon me.
Much have I striven to sing the same,
Brother of beast and tree;
Yet when the stars catch me alone
Never a linnet sings—
And the blood of a man is a bitter voice
And cries for foolish things.

Not for me be the vaunt of woe;
Was not I from a boy
Vowed with the helmet and spear and spur
To the blood-red banner of joy?
A man may sing his psalms to a stone,
Pour his blood for a weed,
But the tears of a man are a sudden thing,
And come not of his creed.

Nay, but the earth is kind to me,
Though I cried for a star,
Leaves and grasses, feather and flower,
Cover the foolish scar,

> Prophets and saints and seraphim
> Lighten the load with song,
> And the heart of a man is a heavy load
> For a man to bear along.

Many poets are writing of war these days. But they write of war too self-consciously, they are too sophisticated, too grown-up. They are so busy getting lessons from the war, describing its moral and social significance, that they have nothing to say about the actual facts of battle. But Chesterton's war poems are splendid primitive things, full of the thunder of crashing arms, of courage and of faith. I think that his "Lepanto" is without an equal among the war poems of the century. It begins as follows:

LEPANTO

White founts falling in the Courts of the sun,
And the Soldan of Byzantium is smiling as they
    run;
There is laughter like the fountains in that face of
    all men feared,
It stirs the forest darkness, the darkness of his
    beard,
It curls the blood-red crescent, the crescent of his
    lips,
For the inmost sea of all the earth is shaken with his
    ships.

They have dared the white republics up the capes
    of Italy,
They have dashed the Adriatic round the Lion of
    the Sea,
And the Pope has cast his arms abroad for agony
    and loss,
And called the kings of Christendom for swords
    about the Cross.
The cold queen of England is looking in the glass;
The shadow of the Valois is yawning at the Mass;
From evening isles fantastical rings faint the Span-
    ish gun,
And the Lord upon the Golden Horn is laughing in
    the sun.
Dim drums throbbing, in the hills half heard,
Where only on a nameless throne a crownless prince
    has stirred,
Where, from a doubtful seat and half attainted
    stall,
The last knight of Europe takes weapons from the
    wall,
The last and lingering troubadour to whom the bird
    has sung,
That once went singing southward when all the
    world was young.
In that enormous silence, tiny and unafraid,
Comes up along a winding road the noise of the
    Crusade.
Strong gongs groaning as the guns boom far,
Don John of Austria is going to the war,

Stiff flags straining in the night-blasts cold
In the gloom black-purple, in the glint old-gold,
Torchlight crimson on the copper kettle-drums,
Then the tuckets, then the trumpets, then the can-
    non, and he comes.
Don John laughing in the brave beard curles,
Spurning of his stirrups like the thrones of all the
    world,
Holding his head up for a flag of all the free.
Love-light of Spain—hurrah!
Death-light of Africa!
Don John of Austria
Is riding to the sea.
Mahound is in his paradise above the evening star,
(Don John of Austria is going to the war).
He moves a mighty turban on the timeless houri's
    knees,
His turban that is woven of the sunsets and the
    seas.
He shakes the peacock gardens as he rises from his
    ease,
And he strides among the tree-tops and is taller
    than the trees,
And his voice through all the garden is a thunder
    sent to bring
Black Azrael and Ariel and Ammon on the wing.
Giants and the Genii,
Multiplex of wing and eye,
Whose strong obedience broke the sky
When Solomon was king.

FUGITIVE PIECES

If any living poet deserves to be called the laureate of democracy, that poet is Gilbert K. Chesterton. I do not base this statement so much on his serious poems in praise of democracy, as on his light verse. In his gay ballades, full of rollicking humor, we find every now and then a bit of shrewd satire, a devastating criticism of the false leaders, of the hypocrites and tyrants who sit in high places. Better than any other writer of our day, Chesterton knows how to drive his rapier of rhyme to the very heart of hypocrisy and injustice. There is sound social and moral criticism back of the irresistible nonsense of "A Ballade of Suicide":

A BALLADE OF SUICIDE

The gallows in my garden, people say,
Is new and neat and adequately tall.
I tie the noose on in a knowing way
As one that knots his necktie for a ball;
But just as all the neighbours—on the wall—
Are drawing a long breath to shout "Hurray!"
The strangest whim has seized me. . . . After all
I think I will not hang myself to-day.

To-morrow is the time I get my pay—
My uncle's sword is hanging in the hall—
I see a little cloud all pink and grey—
Perhaps the rector's mother will *not* call—

I fancy that I heard from Mr. Gall
That mushrooms could be cooked another way—
I never read the works of Juvenal—
I think I will not hang myself to-day.

The world will have another washing day;
The decadents decay; the pedants pall;
And H. G. Wells has found that children play,
And Bernard Shaw discovered that they squall;
Rationalists are growing rational—
And through thick woods one finds a stream astray,
So secret that the very sky seems small—
I think I will not hang myself to-day.

envoi

Prince, I can hear the trumpet of Germinal,
The tumbrils toiling up the terrible way;
Even to-day your royal head may fall—
I think I will not hang myself to-day.

But the poems which most thoroughly justify
their author's claim to the title of poet are the religious poems, such poems as "The House of
Christmas," "A Hymn for the Church Militant,"
"The Nativity" and "The Wise Men." In the last-
named poem we find Chesterton's love of democracy and his hatred of pretentious scientific dogmatism fully expressed, and we find also the thing

which is the basis of these ideas—his deep and abiding faith.   He writes:

THE WISE MEN

Step softly, under snow or rain,
  To find the place where men can pray;
The way is all so very plain
  That we may lose the way.

Oh, we have learnt to peer and pore
  On tortured puzzles from our youth,
We know all labyrinthine lore,
We are the three wise men of yore,
  And we know all things but the truth.

We have gone round and round the hill,
  And lost the wood among the trees,
And learnt long names for every ill,
And served the mad gods, naming still
  The Furies the Eumenides.

The gods of violence took the veil
  Of vision and philosophy,
The Serpent that brought all men bale,
He bites his own accursed tail,
  And calls himself Eternity.

Go humbly . . . it has hailed and snowed . . .
  With voices low and lanterns lit;

CHESTERTON AND HIS POETRY

So very simple is the road,
   That we may stray from it.

The world grows terrible and white,
   And blinding white the breaking day;
We walk bewildered in the light,
For something is too large for sight,
   And something much too plain to say.

The Child that was ere worlds begun
   (. . . We need but walk a little way,
We need but see a latch undone . . .)
The Child that played with moon and sun
   Is playing with a little hay.

The house from which the heavens are fed,
   The old strange house that is our own,
Where tricks of words are never said,
And Mercy is as plain as bread,
   And Honour is as hard as stone.

Go humbly; humble are the skies,
   And low and large and fierce the Star;
So very near the Manger lies
   That we may travel far.

Hark! Laughter like a lion wakes
   To roar to the resounding plain,
And the whole heaven shouts and shakes,
   For God Himself is born again,

FUGITIVE PIECES

And we are little children walking
Through the snow and rain.

This is indeed the beautiful expression of a beautiful impression; it has in every line the unmistakable glow of noble poetry; it is musical, imaginative, direct, and it is passionately Christian. It is the sort of thing which makes it easy to understand why many people, including, it is said, Mrs. Chesterton, believe that this great humorist, this formidable debater, this brilliant novelist, this sound critic, this accomplished essayist, is, before and above all other things, a poet.

LIONEL JOHNSON, ERNEST DOWSON, AUBREY BEARDSLEY

IN considering that brief and tumultuous period in English literature which is sometimes called The Æsthetic Renaissance, it is inevitable that three figures should stand out with particular vividness. They are Lionel Johnson, Aubrey Beardsley and Ernest Dowson—a great poet, a brilliant, but unbalanced illustrator, and another poet, who wrote a great deal of rubbish and about four poems which are genuine and important contributions to English literature. What is the bond between these men? Why should they be grouped together?

They might be grouped together because they all three were creative artists whose careers, so far as the world knows, ended with the nineteenth century. They might be grouped together because they were animated by the same feeling, a violent reaction against the hideous scientific dogmatism, the deadly materialism of the much vaunted Victorian era. And they might be grouped together because all three were artists, seekers after that real but elusive thing called beauty, a thing which they found at last when they had made their submission to her who is the mother of all learning, all culture and all the arts, the Catholic Church.

And yet, although the fact that their conversion establishes a real and noble connection between these three men of genius, their characters and talents differ greatly. Only one of them—and that one Lionel Johnson—was directly inspired through a considerable period of years by his Catholic Faith. Ernest Dowson, the poet, and Aubrey Beardsley, the artist, became Catholics towards the end of their artistic careers, too late for the Faith to give to their work that purity and strength which are the guarantees of immortality. But Lionel Johnson found his Faith almost as soon as he found his genius, celebrated it in poems of enduring beauty, and left the world a precious heritage of song.

In his book "The Eighteen-Nineties," Mr. Holbrook Jackson has pointed out the significance of the revival of æstheticism which took place in the closing years of the nineteenth century, and has shown that it was symptomatic of a sort of idealistic revolt. The poets and artists were sick of the dogmatic materialism which dominated the mind of England. Huxley and Darwin seemed to have dragged the angels out of Heaven, even to have torn down Heaven itself, and to have put in its place nothing save a dull rational and inhuman scientific theory. Against this scientific dogmatism in matters intellectual and spiritual, and against a sort of bleak smugness in matters moral and social, the young idealists of the eighteen-nineties rebelled. Sometimes the thing which they advocated was cheap and tawdry enough, sometimes it was base and vicious. But they were at any rate in revolt—they had found at last that the religion of science and the morality of merely human convention could not satisfy their hearts and their souls.

And there was another phase to the renaissance of the nineties—it was a romantic adventure. These men were all of them young and ardent. If there had been some brave and noble adventure at hand, they would have undertaken it with song on their lips and laughter in their hearts. They longed to be in the daring minority, to battle for lost causes. Now, this tendency by itself, this ambition lacking a worthy aim is a dangerous thing. So some of these young men fell by the wayside, but others saw before them the great and immortal adventure, forsook their trivial toys and poses and attitudes, and enlisted in the shining army of a King more shamefully ill-used than Charles I, more powerful than Charlemagne.

For Aubrey Beardsley I have the greatest sympathy and admiration. That being the case, let me say that for the honor of his memory I wish that every drawing that he made, every one of those deftly-made arrangements in black and white, might be destroyed. It seems to me that he was of all the men of the eighteen-nineties the one genuine decadent. It is not only in such openly vicious things as the illustrations to Wilde's "Salome" that we find deliberate immorality in intention and expression, there is in all his work, however simple and even noble may be the theme, as for instance his illustrations to Malory's "Morte D'Arthur," a definite and unmistakable perversity, a sure sign of physical, mental and moral sickness.

Aubrey Beardsley's mental and moral sickness at first showed itself only in a contempt for the conventions of art and in especial for the conventions of proportion and prospective. It has sometimes been said that it is as absurd to rebel against the moral law as against the law of gravitation. The first revolt of a consumptive young architectural draughtsman with an extraordinary talent for line was against natural law—against the law of proportion. The first drawings which brought him any notoriety were extraordinary for two things— their admirable draughtsmanship and their deliberate eccentricities of proportion. He drew nothing but monsters—men eight feet tall with microscopic heads, women with arms as long as their entire bodies. The revolt against the moral law came later—the selection of hideously obscene subjects, the painful obsession with sex. Then came the sick boy's discoveries that after all beauty was no more in the weird ugliness he had celebrated than it was in the smug conventions of sentimental Victorian painting. A few weeks before his death Aubrey Beardsley found the immortal abiding place of beauty. Received into the Church, Aubrey Beardsley repented bitterly his misuse of his talents, and plead with his friends to destroy all his immoral drawings, of which he was now thoroughly ashamed. "Burn all my bawdy pictures," he wrote —a dying prayer which his pagan friends utterly disregarded. He had striven to find beauty in sin, and he knew that this seeking was in vain. For now, he had found beauty, now he had learned to see in the lamp which is beauty the light which is God.

I have said that Aubrey Beardsley was the only

true decadent of all the literary and artistic rebels of the eighteen-nineties. Certainly no intelligent person can call Ernest Dowson a decadent. It is true that there have been critics, such as Mr. Blakie Murdoch, who have tried to throw a halo of wickedness over this unfortunate young poet, to make him seem to be a sort of English Paul Verlaine. But Victor Plarr, who knew him intimately for many years, has told us that except for the tendency to drink too much, which was one of the causes of his death, Ernest Dowson was a simple, wholesome young man, who smoked large black cigars and was fond of playing practical jokes on his friends.

Ernest Dowson's religious poems have never seemed to me to be particularly convincing. I will read you one of the best of them and then tell you why it does not seem to me to ring true. It is called "Nuns of the Perpetual Adoration."

NUNS OF THE PERPETUAL ADORATION

BY ERNEST DOWSON

Calm, sad, secure; behind high convent walls,
   These watch the sacred lamp, these watch and
      pray:
And it is one with them when evening falls,
   And one with them the cold return of day.

JOHNSON, DOWSON AND BEARDSLEY

These heed not time; their nights and days they
    make
  Into a long, returning rosary,
Whereon their lives are threaded for Christ's sake:
  Meekness and vigilance and chastity.

A vowed patrol, in silent companies,
  Life-long they keep before the living Christ.
In the dim church, their prayers and penances
  Are fragrant incense to the Sacrificed.

Outside, the world is wild and passionate;
  Man's weary laughter and his sick despair
Entreat at their impenetrable gate:
  They heed no voices in their dream of prayer.

They saw the glory of the world displayed;
  They saw the bitter of it, and the sweet;
They knew the roses of the world would fade,
  And be trod under by the hurrying feet.

Therefore they rather put away desire,
  And crossed their hands and came to sanctuary;
And veiled their heads and put on coarse attire:
  Because their comeliness was vanity.

And there they rest; they have serene insight
  Of the illuminating dawn to be:
Mary's sweet Star dispels for them the night,
  The proper darkness of humanity.

Calm, sad, secure; with faces worn and mild:
  Surely their choice of vigil is the best?
Yea! for our roses fade, the world is wild;
  But there, beside the altar, there, is rest.

Now, this is a very beautiful poem. But there is
nothing in it which might not have been written by
a Protestant. And there is one note in it which
seems to me to be absolutely contrary to the Catholic idea of the religious life—and that is the note of
melancholy. Ernest Dowson insists that the nuns
are sad as well as calm and secure, he insists upon
the fact that their faces are "worn and mild." Also
he apparently thinks of the convent as a place of
inaction, instead of as a place of ordered and ener-
getic activity. Therefore, this poem, beautiful as
it is, seems to me to be in no way Catholic in spirit
or in expression.

But while I do not feel that the authenticity of
Ernest Dowson's Catholicity can be proved by his
deliberately religious poems, I do think that in
nearly every poem which this so-called decadent
wrote it is possible to find indications if not of piety,
at least of normality, sanity, wholesomeness and
virtue.

There are, and there have always been since sin
first came into the world, genuine decadents. That

is, there have been writers who have devoted all their energies and talents to the cause of evil, who have consistently and sincerely opposed Christian morality, and zealously endeavored to make the worst appear the better cause. But every poet who lays a lyric wreath at a heathen shrine, who sings the delights of immorality, or hashish, or suicide, or mayhem, is not a decadent: often he is merely weak-minded. The true decadent, to paraphrase a famous saying, wears his vices lightly, like a flower. He really succeeds in making vice seem picturesque and amusing and even attractive.

Now, this is exactly what Ernest Dowson never could do. He was a member, it will be remembered, of that little band of æsthetic poets which was called The Rhymers Club. With them he spent certain evenings at the Cheshire Cheese, and there he drank absinthe. This is a significant and symbolic fact. Not in some ominous Parisian cellar, but beneath the beamed ceiling of a most British inn, still stained with smoke from the pipe of Dr. Samuel Johnson, among thick mutton chops and tankards of musty ale, in a cloud of sweet-scented steam that rose from the parted crust of the magnificent pigeon pie, Ernest Dowson drank absinthe.

There is splendid symbolism in Ernest Dowson's

act of drinking absinthe in the Cheshire Cheese. The wickedness in his poems and his prose sketches is always as affected and incongruous as is that pallid medicine in any honest tavern.

He tried hard to be pagan. In the manner of Mr. Swinburne, he exclaims: "Goddess the laughter-loving, Aphrodite, Aphrodite, befriend! Let me have peace of. thee, truce of thee, golden one, send!" And not even Mr. Swinburne ever wrote lines so absolutely unconvincing. He said "I go where the wind blows, Chloe, and am not sorry at all." And from this lyric no one can fail to get the impression that the poet was very sorry indeed.

Ernest Dowson was an accomplished artist in words, a delicate sensitive and graceful genius, but he was no more fitted to be a pagan than to be a policeman. And so, in his best known poems, he uses all the pagan properties, all the splendors of sin's pageantry, but his theme, his overmastering thoughts, is a soul-shaking lament for his stained faithfulness, for his treason to the Catholic ideal of chastity.

Ernest Dowson could not write poems that really were pagan. He was not a true decadent. And for this undoubtedly he now is thanking God. He had his foolish hours: he sometimes misused his gift of song. But—and this is the important thing about it—he did not know how to misuse it successfully. The real Ernest Dowson was not the picturesque vagabond about whom Mr. Blackie Murdoch has written, but the man who with all his heart praised "meekness and vigilance and chastity," who "was faithful" in his pathetic ineffective fashion, who knew at last the fidelity of his eternal Mother, who, in Katherine Brégy's beautiful words, "laid his broken body in consecrated ground and followed his bruised soul, with her pitiful asperging prayers."

In considering the eccentricities of "The Savoy" and "The Yellow Book," in considering all the literary and artistic artificialities of the eighteen-nineties, it seems to me that one real value of the cult of peacocks and green carnations, of artificial paganism and sophisticated loveliness, is that it furnishes a splendidly contrasting background for the white genius of Lionel Johnson.

This aristocratic and wealthy young Oxford graduate might so easily have become an æsthete and nothing more! His environment, many of his friendships, even his discipleship, as it may be called, to Walter Pater might naturally be expected to cause him to develop into a mere dilet-

tante, interested only in delicate and superficial
beauty, having, by way of moral code, an earnest
desire to live up to his blue chine.

Instead, what was Lionel Johnson? He was a
sound and accomplished scholar, writing Latin
hymns that for their grace and authentic ecclesias-
tical style might stand beside those of Adam of St.
Victor or of St. Bernard himself. Nor was he less
deft in his manipulation of the style of the classical
authors, as many graceful lines show. And this,
remember, was at a time when Latin was most absolutely a dead language to most young English
poets, whose attention was given entirely to the picturesque attractions of the Parisian *argot* beloved
of the decadents.

The æsthetic movement of the eighteen-nineties
was merely a search for beauty—merely a revolt
against Victorian agnosticism and materialism.
Johnson found the adventure which all the young
poets and artists were seeking; he knew that the
only answer to their question was the Catholic Faith.

The atmosphere of the literary world in which
he lived seems to have had no effect upon Lionel
Johnson's mind and soul. He was "of the centre"
not "of the movement." He gladly accepted the
gracious traditions of English poetry. He fol-

lowed the time-hallowed conventions of his craft as faithfully as did Tennyson. He had no desire to toss Milton's wreath either to Whitman or to Baudelaire.

But these virtues are perhaps chiefly negative. Almost the same thing might be said of many poets, of the late Stephen Phillips, for example, who certainly was an honest traditionalist, uninfluenced by decadence or æstheticism. But Lionel Johnson had also (what Stephen Phillips lacked) a great and beautiful philosophy. And his philosophy was true. He was so fortunate as to hold the Catholic Faith. This Faith inspired his best poems, shines through them and makes them, as the word is used, immortal.

While Lionel Johnson was not exclusively a devotional and religious poet, the theme which he sang with the most splendid passion and the most consummate art was the Catholic Church. This was the great influence in his life; it is to this that his poetry owes most of its enduring beauty. But there were other influences, there were other things which claimed, to a less degree, his devotion. One of these is Ireland.

Lionel Johnson's chivalrous loyalty to Ireland was not without its quaint humor. He was descended from the severe and brutal general who savagely put down the insurrection of 1798. But he by no means shared his ancestor's views in Irish matters; he was an enthusiastic advocate of Irish freedom and a devoted lover of everything Irish.

Although he hailed with delight the revival of ancient Celtic customs and the ancient Celtic language, Lionel Johnson was far from being what we have come to call a neo-Celt. He did not spend his time in writing elaborately annotated chants in praise of Cuchulain and Deidre and Oengus, and other creatures of legend; the attempt to reëstablish Ireland's ancient paganism seemed to him singularly unintelligent. He saw that the greatest glory of Ireland is her fidelity to the Catholic Faith, a fidelity which countless cruel persecutions have only strengthened. And so when he wrote of Ireland's dead, he did not see them entering into some Ossianic land of dead warriors. Instead he wrote:

> For their loyal love, nought less,
>   Than the stress of death sufficed:
> Now with Christ, in blessedness,
>   Triumph they, imparadised.

Similarly, in what is generally considered to be his greatest poem, the majestic and passionate "Ireland," his most joyous vision is that of the "Bright souls of Saints, glad choirs of intercession from the Gael," and he concludes with this splendid prayer:

O Rose! O Lily! O Lady full of grace!
  O Mary Mother! O Mary Maid! hear thou.
Glory of Angels! Pity, and turn they face,
  Praying thy Son, even as we pray thee now,
For thy dear sake to set thine Ireland free:
  Pray thou thy Little Child!
Ah! who can help her, but in mercy He?
  Pray then, pray thou for Ireland, Mother mild!
O heart of Mary! Pray the Sacred Heart:
His, at Whose word depart
  Sorrows and hates, home to Hell's waste and
    wild.

Lionel Johnson was, as Miss Louise Imogen Guiney has written, "a tower of wholesomeness in the decadence which his short life spanned." His purely secular poems are best when his Catholic Faith, seemingly without his willing it, unexpectedly shines out in a splendor of radiant phrases. And of all his poems, those which constitute his most important contributions to literature, are those which are directly the fruit of his religious experiences or of his love for Ireland. He was not so great a poet as Francis Thompson. He never wrote a poem that will stand comparison with "The Hound of Heaven" or the "Orient Ode." But the sum of the beauty in all his work is great, and his poetry is, on the whole, more companionable than that of Francis Thompson; it is more human, more personal, more intimate.

And to at least two of Lionel Johnson's poems, the adjective "great" may, by every sound critical standard, safely be applied. One of these is the "Dark Angel," a masterly study of the psychology of temptation, written in stanzas that glow with feeling, that are the direct and passionate utterance of the poet's soul, and yet are as polished and accurate as if their author's only purpose had been to make a thing of beauty. The other is "Te Martyrum Candidatus," a poem which may without question be given its place in any anthology which contains "Burning Babe," "The Kings," and Crashaw's "Hymn to St. Teresa." It has seemed to me that these brave and beautiful lines, which have for their inspiration the love of God, and echo with their chiming syllables the hoof-beats of horses bearing knights to God's battles, might serve as a fitting epitaph for the accomplished scholar, the true poet, the noble and kindly Catholic gentleman who wrote them.

SWINBURNE AND FRANCIS THOMPSON

I FEEL a certain diffidence in approaching the subject of Francis Thompson before such an audience as this. For I know that there are many among you who could teach me much about that great poet, the modern laureate of the Catholic Church. I suppose that many of you have studied the profound philosophy of "From the Night of Forebeing," "The Mistress of Vision" and "The Hound of Heaven," have curiously examined the beautiful verbal intricacies of "Sister Songs" and "The Orient Ode," and are familiar with the triumphs and the tragedies of Francis Thompson's brief life.

But there may be some among you to whom Francis Thompson is little more than a name. To such let me say that Francis Thompson was born of Catholic parents in Lancashire, England, in 1859, that he died, fortified by the last rites of the Church he loved, at the age of forty-eight, that most of his life was spent in poverty and ill-health, that he was subject to terrible and persistent temptations, but remained faithful to the Church, and made in the Church's honor some of the greatest poems in the English language. I compare him to a contemporary poet, Algernon Charles Swinburne, chiefly because Swinburne was the poet of Paganism as Francis Thompson was the poet of Catholicity, because their careers present interesting resemblances as well as interesting contrasts, and because both are what is called "Victorian" poets.

Now, in this connection let me ask you if you ever seriously considered the advantages of living in a Republic, of living, for example, in the United States of America instead of in England? There is, for example, the recurrent excitement of changing the president once every four years, of having every so often a new chief executive on whom to vent your enthusiastic affection or your enthusiastic loathing. A president is a wonderful safety-valve for the pent-up feelings of a nation. The suffrage, the right to vote, must be a golden privilege indeed, otherwise so many members of the wiser sex would not pursue it with such zeal and devotion.

But the advantage of living in a Republic to which I desire particularly to call your attention this afternoon is the advantage of escaping from the custom of calling periods of artistic and literary endeavor after the sovereigns who happened to rule during them. You never hear James Whitcomb Riley or Edwin Markham spoken of as Wilsonian poets. But you do hear Ben Jonson called an Elizabethan poet, which is just as absurd. You never hear Bryant and Whittier called poets of the Lincoln period. But you do hear such utterly dissimilar poets as Algernon Charles Swinburne and Francis Thompson spoken of as Victorian poets.

Why is this? Why is the Elizabethan era? Why should the age that glowed with the deathless flames of Shakespeare's genius, that echoed with Ben Jonson's lyric laughter, that was pierced by the poignant music of Robert Southwell, the martyred Jesuit poet, be named after Elizabeth, the persecutor of the saints, the vain and selfish and cruel woman who then occupied England's throne, to England's lasting shame?

And why are we to-day considering, in Swinburne and Francis Thompson, two Victorian poets? Why Victorian? Of course, Queen Victoria was a good wife and mother, a noble gentlewoman. I think that we all like everything that we know about Queen Victoria except perhaps her politics.

But why should the name of this estimable woman be used to designate the intellectual and spiritual life of the time during which she ruled, a life from which she was as remote as was the Queen of Sheba? Why should we give the placid name Victorian to that time of violent sin and violent virtue, of passionate infidelity and passionate faith, that time which produced the Darwinian theory, and the Oxford Movement, which produced the cruel reign of dogmatic science and the Catholic renascence, which produced the poetry of Algernon Charles Swinburne and the poetry of Francis Thompson?

The combination of these two names may strike you as unusual. You know that Swinburne was what is called a Pagan, that he hated all forms of Christianity and especially the Catholic Church. You know also that Francis Thompson was the Church's poet-laureate, the greatest Catholic poet of modern times. And you wonder why Swinburne and Francis Thompson should be mentioned in the same breath.

Well, great as are the differences between these poets, the resemblances are striking. It is true that when Swinburne was at the height of his fame, Francis Thompson was running errands and holding horses in the London streets, his genius practically unknown. Yet he was famous before Swinburne's death, and there are other points of contact beside that of time between this militant pagan and this militant Christian.

In the first place, both were poets. Both had genuine talent, and both had a strong desire to do the work of the poet, that is, to find beauty and to bind beauty with a chain of linked rhyme.

Now the poet's search for beauty often is difficult, and it was especially difficult in London in the latter days of the nineteenth century. All the poets were seeking for beauty, but the scientists had been industriously trying to drive beauty out of the world. Of course, they had not succeeded, any more than the French Atheist succeeded a few years ago in carrying out his blasphemous threat of putting out that light in the heavens. But they had thrown a veil over the face of beauty, and made beauty hard to see except for those who looked with the strong eyes of faith.

How the poets worried! Where had beauty flown? Browning thought that beauty was in humanity. So he searched for beauty in humanity, and in his search made many interesting and noble poems. Tennyson, that magnificent artist in words, thought that beauty was somewhere in evolution. And he at last descended to the most supine of intellectual attitudes, his philosophy being merely that somehow good would be the final goal of all, that everything would come out all right in the end. And he uttered the most absurd statement ever made by any poet in the history of the world when he said "There lies more faith in honest doubt, believe me, than in half the creeds."

All the poets were seeking after beauty. When Swinburne, full of Greek and Latin and talent and conceit, left Oxford University to begin a military career, he was seeking for beauty. And when Francis Thompson was selling matches and shoestrings in the London gutters, he was seeking for beauty.

Swinburne knew that the life around him was dull and materialistic. The scientists had said that the old ethical and spiritual values were dead. There could be no beauty in religion, for the scientists had killed religion, putting up in its place their own artificial dogma. Beauty and light had gone out of life.

So Swinburne decided, logically enough, that since beauty was not in his own land and age, he must seek it in the ages that had gone before. So he wrote not of modern scientific, dull, Victorian London, but of ancient Venice, of ancient Rome, of ancient Greece. He lamented the departure of Venus and Apollo and Dionysus and all the old gods and goddesses, and the loss of the glories of the spacious classic days.

But Swinburne failed. Musical as are his rhymes and rhythms, lofty as was his imagination, he failed. He failed to write convincingly of medieval Rome and ancient Venice because he could not understand what made these cities beautiful and great—their faith. He failed to write convincingly of ancient Greece because he could never be that rare and in its way splendid thing, an honest pagan.

No one can be a real pagan nowadays. Swinburne is not to be blamed because he failed to be a real pagan, but because he tried to be a pagan. The ancient Greeks who lived before the time of Christ were brave and simple men, their chief virtues were courage, patriotism, obedience to the law, democracy and zeal for art. These virtues were in time taken over and multiplied by the Catholic Church, which has preserved all of pagan culture that deserved preservation. Swinburne rejected these virtues, probably thinking them to be Christian innovations, and the pagans of whom he wrote were sensual, decadent things, like the degenerate Greeks who lived in the days of Roman supremacy. And Swinburne finally reached his true level in the poem in which he speaks by the mouth of Julian the Apostate, the poor maniac who rejected Christianity and struggled vainly to restore the worship of the legendary gods of his heathen ancestors.

Francis Thompson, like Swinburne, sought for beauty. And Francis Thompson found beauty. Francis Thompson found beauty because he knew where to look. He found beauty in prosaic scientific modern London, he found beauty in the city streets. He found beauty right around the corner, in a certain little Church around the corner which is also the big Church around the world. He found beauty where she is and always will be, in the Catholic faith.

Swinburne felt his lack of faith. He bitterly resented the veil that his infidelity had put between himself and beauty. And therefore he attacked faith, and railed with all the venom of a disappointed man against Christ, his Saints and His Church.

Swinburne longed for the days of pagan license and revelry, when Pan and Apollo dwelt with man. Francis Thompson knew that God was with man, that no street was so humble, no house so poor as not to know the tread of His feet. Instead of longing for a return of the old imaginary gods, he saw the beauty of God evident in such harsh thoroughfares as Charing Cross, and brooding even over the muddy waters of the Thames. He wrote:

THE KINGDOM OF GOD

The angels keep their ancient places,
   Turn but a stone and start a wing,
'Tis ye, 'tis your estranged faces
   That miss the many splendoured thing.

But when so sad thou canst not sadder
   Cry:—and upon thy so sore loss
Shall shine the traffic of Jacob's ladder
   Pitched between Heaven and Charing Cross.

Yea, in the night, my Soul, my daughter,
   Cry,—clinging Heaven by the hems;
And lo, Christ walking on the water
   Not of Gennesareth but Thames!

A dangerous test of a poet's genius is to be found in his attitude towards the simplest and smallest things. It is for this reason that any poet of talent may safely write about a mountain or a waterfall or a sunset, but only a very great poet should ever

write about children. The poets know this, and
in spite of his paganism and sophistication Swinburne often tried to prove his genius by making
excursions into the enchanted land of childhood.
He wrote one poem which he considered a very important achievement, reprinting it in many editions of his poetry. And in that poem Swinburne
did accomplish something well worthy of accom-
plishment, he expressed an interesting and beautiful
idea. Now it would be absurd to take this poem of
Swinburne's and compare it with one of Francis
Thompson's masterpieces, such as "The Hound of
Heaven." But it surely is fair to compare it to a
poem by Francis Thompson on the same theme.

You must consider how it is that a poet writes a
poem. There are said to be poets who are struck
on the head by a great inspiration, and let that inspiration trickle down through the shoulder and
arm and out the end of a pen upon a piece of paper.
There are said to be such poets, although in my
rather extensive observation of poets I have never
met one. The usual method is for a poet to medi-
tate on a subject, to set down on paper all the most
beautiful ideas which his subject suggests to him.

Well, let us imagine Swinburne confronted by
the miracle of childhood. Knowing that his repu-

tation must stand or fall by this attempt, he endeavors to record all the splendid emotions and noble comparisons which childhood suggests to him. And what is the result? What is the climax of thought in his poem? The climax is this: Swinburne says that the baby about whom he is writing, who happens to be wearing a plush cap, looks like a moss rose bud in its soft sheath.

This is a pleasant idea. Undoubtedly it pleased the baby's mother and the baby herself when she grew up. But these are scarcely the words that shall tremble on the lips of time.

Francis Thompson was great enough to do the obvious thing. When he was drawing inspiration from the miracle of childhood, he did not think about plush caps and moss roses. Instead, he did the most natural and the most beautiful thing. He thought about the Infant Jesus. Childhood to him suggested Him Who made childhood Divine. And in "Ex Ore Infantium" he gave that thought immortal expression.

But in comparing the plush cap of the baby to a moss rose, Swinburne did not think he had said the last word on the subject. As the result of prolonged meditation on childhood, he produced another poem in which he really did accomplish something remarkable. He found a rhyme for "babe."

Now, I doubt if any of you know the rhyme for "babe," unless you happen to be familiar with this poem of Swinburne's or with those of Chaucer, who also used this word. There is such a word and Swinburne ingeniously introduces it towards the end of his poem. He writes:

> Babe, if rhyme be none
>   For that small sweet word,
> Babe, the sweetest one
>   Ever heard,
> Right it is and sweet
>   Rhyme should not keep true
> Time with such a sweet
>   Thing as you . . .
> . . . None can tell in metre
>   Fit for ears on earth
> What sweet star grew sweeter
>   At your birth.
> Wisdom doubts what may be;
>   Hope with smile sublime
> Trusts, but neither, baby
>   Knows the rhyme.
> Wisdom lies down lonely;
>   Hope keeps watch from far;
> None but one seer only
>   Sees the star.

> Love alone, with yearning
>   Heart for astrolabe
> Takes the star's height, burning
>   O'er the babe.

Compare this, not with Francis Thompson's "Hound of Heaven," but with another poem on childhood, and from that poem decide which of the two poets had the real inspiration. Compare it with Francis Thompson's poem to his god-child. In this he imagines himself as having died, and he imagines that the little boy has died too. So he gives the little boy a kind of working plan of Heaven—he tells him where he may find him after he goes to Heaven. He writes:

And when, immortal mortal, droops your head,
And you, the child of deathless song, are dead;
Then, as you search with unaccustomed glance
The ranks of Paradise for my countenance,
Turn not your tread along the Uranian sod,
Among the bearded counsellors of God;
For if in Eden as on earth are we
I sure shall keep a younger company:
Pass where beneath their ranged ganfalons
The starry cohorts shake their shielded suns,
The dreadful mass of their enridged spears;
Pass where majestical the Eternal peers
The stately choice of the great saintdom meet,—

[265]

A silvern congregation, globed complete
In sandalled shadow of the Triune feet:
Pass by where wait, your poet wayfarer,
Your cousin clusters, emulous to share
With you the roseal lightnings burning mid their
    hair;
Pass the crystalline sea, the Lampads Seven:—
Look for me in the nurseries of Heaven.

I have said that Francis Thompson was great and simple enough to do the obvious thing. Take the mere matter of how to act and what to say in regard to a crucifix, for example. When that admirable poet Dante Gabriel Rossetti was before a crucifix, or had it in mind as the theme of a poem, he would admire the carving, and write a colorful romantic ballad about the man who made it, the man who sold it, the people through whose hands it had passed. The result would be a beautiful poem, but it would be elaborate, artificial, the result of ingenious effort. When Swinburne was before a crucifix, he was reminded of the false delights for which he longed, and which he thought Christianity had driven from the world. So he would rave and blaspheme against the crucifix and all that it represented—producing verse that is technically excellent, but artificial and unnatural. But when

Francis Thompson had a crucifix before him or in mind, he would do the simplest and most natural thing in the world. He would say his prayers. And because he was a genius he said them in words that are, as we use the term of literature, immortal.

A NOTE ON THOMAS HARDY

OF Elizabeth-Jane who is the heroine of "The Mayor of Casterbridge," if heroine this tale may be said to have, we learn that "she did not cease to wonder at the persistence of the unforeseen, when the one to whom such unbroken tranquillity had been accorded in the adult stage was she whose youth had seemed to teach that happiness was but the occasional episode in a general drama of pain." This is a rather Jacobean sentence, in form not typical of Hardy, but in thought it is greatly significant. It is likely that Hardy himself wondered at the happiness in which he left Elizabeth-Jane, reassuring himself perhaps by the conviction that her "unbroken tranquillity" was the exception which proved the rule her youth had taught her.

For it cannot be denied that according to the Hardy philosophy, implicit in his tales and explicit in his poems, sorrow is the rule and joy the exception. In no other writing is he more clearly a fatalist than in "The Mayor of Casterbridge"; in no other book does he urge more unmistakably his belief that men and women are but helpless puppets in the hands of mischievous fate, that good-will and courage and honesty are brittle weapons for humanity's defense.

The evident fact that Thomas Hardy is a fatalist is responsible for the common and absurd idea that he is a pagan. Now, there is no philosophy—with the exception of the robust and joyous philosophy of the Middle Ages—with which Hardy's philosophy contrasts more strongly than it does with paganism, that is, with the pagan philosophy of the spacious classic day. When we speak of a pagan of ancient Greece or a pagan of ancient Rome we have in mind a brave patriotic man, with a vivid sense of the responsibilities and privileges of citizenship, and the habit of making the most of life, of enjoying to the full the years allowed him on earth. This last characteristic rose from the pagan fatalism, the belief that man should make sure of such visible and tangible delights as were available, because there was no counting on the possibility of happiness or even of existence after death. This was the state of mind which succeeded the earlier romantic polytheism, and was the natural successor of a religious system which attributed to the gods power over mankind but neither love nor justice.

So the typical fatalism was materialistic; it was based, of course, upon despair, but its manifestations were not desperate. Rather there was a general conspiracy of joy, not dissimilar to that of a popular religious cult which arose in the United States during the last half century. Disease and sorrow and death were to be generally ignored; mankind was expected to eat, drink and be merry, and good manners required silence as to the explanatory "for to-morrow we die."

However hollow may have been mirth of the pagan fatalists, it was at any rate loud and general. And there can be no doubt that by a kind of self-hypnosis these fatalists were able to give their joy a convincingness and a continuity—they "were always drunken," in Baudelaire's sense. Artificial and in essence tragic as was their state of mind, he would be a false historian who pictured these pagan fatalists as people obsessed with the idea of death and the unkindness of the gods; as holding with anything like unanimity the belief that "happiness was but the occasional episode in a general drama of pain."

But this is Hardy's dominant idea; it is a belief on which he insists with a propagandist enthusiasm which sometimes mars the artistic value of his work.

A NOTE ON THOMAS HARDY

No Scotch or English members of some stricter off-shoot of a strict Calvinistic sect ever was more firm-ly convinced that this earth is a vale of tears, or more eager to spread this belief. Every writer, I think, deals with the characters who are his crea-tions as he imagines God to deal with mankind. This is why literary criticism is closer to theology than to any other science; this is why we cannot claim to understand any writer unless we know what he thinks about God. And the God of Hardy's belief, as indicated in his long succession of stories and poems, is no more the remote, in-different, sensuous, self-sufficient Deity of the pagan fatalist than he is the loving and omnipotent Father of.true Christian belief. Instead he is the stern, avenging Deity of the Hebrews, without pity, accessible to no intercessors, the Deity whom we find to-day fearfully worshiped by adherents of the bleakest forms of Puritanism. It would be a misnomer to call Hardy's philosophy a Christian fatalism, but it is a fatalism which is the basis of the religious systems of many who since 1517 have professed and called themselves Christians.

I am frequently impressed, as I read Hardy, with what I may call the evangelical cast of his mind. He is so intent on announcing his discovery that mankind is fallible, unhappy, helpless, undesirable. The people of Hardy's stories are so virtueless, for the most part, that the reader can readily believe that Hardy is determined to show that they deserve no pity from the extraordinary Deity who is also a creature of Hardy's imagination, and that in his own way the novelist (like his greatest Puritan predecessor in literature) is trying to "justify the ways of God toward man." And "The Mayor of Casterbridge," with its lovely pictures of Wessex hills and valleys and its most unlovely pictures of Wessex men and women, irresistibly recalls lines from a certain popular evangelical hymn—the lines which tell of a place "where every prospect pleases and only man is vile."

Hardy is a true realist in that he reports faithfully the habits and manners of people with whom he is familiar, and in that—unlike Mr. Dreiser and other claimants to the title realist—he has humor and admits it to his chronicles. Also he admits good impulses to the lives he creates, although his philosophy seldom lets him cause these impulses to be translated into successful action. He is poet enough to have a sense of beauty and humor inherent in phrases. "But I know that 'a's a banded teetotaler," says Solomon Longways, "and that if any of his men be ever so little overtook by a drop he's down upon 'em as stern as the Lord upon the jovial Jews." And what living poet could write a simpler and more moving study of the immemorial subject, death, than Mother Cuxsom's brief elegy on Mrs. Henchard? "Well, poor soul, she's helpless to hinder that or anything now. And all her shining keys will be took from her, and her cupboards opened; and little things a' didn't wish seen, anybody will see; and her wishes and ways will all be as nothing."

A student of literary motives can easily trace the working of Hardy's philosophy in this book—can see it guiding the novelist's pen, changing his purposes, forcing him to deal harshly, sometimes, with characters whom a writer must come to love as a father his children. Was not Matthew Henchard's rehabilitation to be complete, and the tale to end with a prosperous reunited family? Probably, but Thomas Hardy (unlike Victor Hugo when he handled a similar plot in "Les Miserables") had his monster theory to reckon with. So Elizabeth-Jane must be Newson's child, Lucette must maleficently tangle lives, and Henchard must die in a road-side hut. And even the goldfinch must starve in its paper-covered cage.

And how Hardy enjoys the moments when he escapes his obsession! He had as much fun when Henchard and Farfrae wrestled on the top floor of the granary as Blackmore did in the Homeric fisticuffs of "Lorna Doone." When Hardy dressed up Lucetta and sent her out to plead with Henchard he had the same sporting excitement that Thackeray had when he prepared Becky Sharp for her conquests. At such times Hardy seems momentarily to accept the existence of free will, with its tremendous dramatic possibilities. These are his moments of greatest creative power, of highest poetry, of clearest discernment. They occur more frequently and they last longer in his latest writings. The War has seen to that.

MADISON JULIUS CAWEIN

(1865-1914)

A MERICA has had two great poets of nature
—two men called to the task of reflecting in
a mirror of words the beauty of meadow and forest.
One of these was William Cullen Bryant. The
other was Madison Julius Cawein.

As Bryant drew his inspiration from the wooded
hills and fertile valleys of his native New England,
so Madison Cawein drew his from the meadows of
the South, especially those of Kentucky. The term
"nature poet" has been used in derision of some
writers who lavish sentimental adulation upon
every bird and flower, who pretend an admiration
for things of which they have no real understanding. But Madison Cawein knew what he was writing about; he had an amazing, we might say a perilous, intimacy with nature. And he had no vague
love for all nature—he knew too much for that.
True, he knew nature in her delicate and in her
splendid aspect—he saw the barberry redden in the

lanes, he feasted his eyes on "the orange and amber of the marigold, the terra-cottas of the zinnia flowers," he learned lovely secrets from whippoorwill, swallow, and cricket, and he could see drowsy Summer rocking the world to sleep in her kindly arms. But also he knew (with a knowledge which only Algernon Blackwood among contemporary writers has equaled) that nature has her cruel and terrible aspects. He knew that the daily life of bird and beast—yes, and the daily life of flower and tree—is as much a tragedy as a comedy. So (in the sonnet-sequence he wrote by the Massachusetts shore in 1911) he saw a certain grove as "a sad room, devoted to the dead"; he felt the relentlessness of the ocean mists invading the shore; he saw an autumn branch staining a pool like a blur of blood; he made us share his genuine terror of deserted millstreams where "the cardinal-flower, in the sun's broad beam, with sudden scarlet takes you by surprise," and of dark and menacing swamps, ominous with trembling moss, purple-veined pitcher-plants and wild grass trailing over the bank like the hair of a drowned girl. His studies of nature were accurate enough to satisfy any botanist—Miss Jessie B. Rittenhouse has said that one might explore the Kentucky woods and fields with a volume of

Cawein's poems as a handbook and identify many a lowly and exquisite bower first recognized in song. But his poems were not mere catalogues of natural beauties, any more than they were sentimental idealizations of them. They were, to repeat a phrase, reflections of nature, reflections painted rather than photographed, but interpreted rather than romanticized.

Madison Cawein had not long to wait for the recognition which he enjoyed throughout his life. Born on March 23rd, 1865, in Louisville, Kentucky, and educated in the high school of his native city, he published his first book, "Blooms of the Berry," in 1887. "The Triumph of Music" followed in 1888, and soon after its publication Mr. William Dean Howells wrote of the young Southern poet words that brought him to the attention of a large audience, words that applied as truly to his posthumous book, "The Cup of Comus," as to the rhymes of his boyhood. In the *North American Review,* Mr. Howells wrote:

"He has the gift, in a measure that I do not think surpassed in any poet, of touching some smallest or commonest thing in nature and making it live from the manifold associations in which we have our

[277]

being, and glow thereafter with an inextinguishable beauty."

From 1887 to the time of his death, scarcely a year passed that did not see the publication of a new book of poems by Madison Cawein. Of course, this caused him to be accused of writing too much, of giving the world poems written hastily and carelessly. There was some justice in this accusation; undoubtedly he would have written better poems if he had written fewer. Mr. H. Houston Peckham, of Purdue University, in an article which appeared in the *South Atlantic Quarterly* soon after Cawein's death, told a story which is significant. The poet was about to destroy one of his lyrics. A friend rescued it and sent it to a magazine. When it appeared in print, it was shown to Cawein, who failed to recognize it as his own work. He had utterly forgotten it in the course of a few months.

Now, for a poet to forget the children of his own fancy is a sign that he is writing too much. And yet Madison Cawein was not so prolific as a list of his more than a score of volumes would indicate. For many of his books contained poems that had already appeared between covers—this is true of the Macmillan volume called "Poems" and of many others. He seemed to desire to produce a book annually—but fortunately for his art he did not believe it necessary that every volume should contain only new poems.

In one of the most famous of his essays, Ruskin wrote:

"It is, I hope, now made clear to the reader in all respects that the pathetic fallacy is powerful only so far as it is pathetic, feeble so far as it is fallacious, and, therefore, that the dominion of Truth is entire, over this as over every other natural and just state of the human mind."

Madison Cawein was a loyal subject of Truth, the accuracy of his descriptions of nature has seldom been called into question. As to the pathetic fallacy and his relation to it—that might be the subject of an interesting study. At any rate it may be said that he seldom indulged in that common and thoroughly normal fallacy by which the poet sees nature weep because of his own sorrow or smile because of his own joy. Instead, he was filled with the gloom native to the swamp which he beheld, or with mirth that he caught from the lyric ecstasy of the dawn.

He was a sympathetic student of humanity, as every true poet must be, and he resented the statement that mankind had no place in his poetic vision.

But he was at his best when he wrote not of reasonable humanity but of the world of animal and vegetable things that have no reason but have, to the poet, qualities stranger and more interesting than reason. He wrote well of a ploughman, but better of the field in which the ploughman worked. He wrote well of a house full of men and women and children, but better of an empty house with its myrtle run wild, its paths hidden by flowering grass, and swallows flying through its broken windows. He subordinated himself to wild nature, letting her speak to the world through him, instead of merely going to her for metaphors appropriate to his own emotional experiences. And this, while it resulted in beautiful poetry, was a dangerous thing to do. "Nature, poor stepdame, cannot slake my drouth," said another poet, "never did any milk of hers once bless my thirsting mouth." Madison Cawein got, it seems, little gratitude from Nature, although to do her honor he had curiously distorted the true vision of man's place in the universe. When his frail body was put in the frozen earth a few years ago, it seemed to many of his friends and critics that he had died at the beginning of a new phase of his genius, that his latest poems, vague and tentative as some of them were, showed that he was looking at the world with a new sense of proportion, and that hereafter his whole scheme of things would be differently arranged—man being the center of the visible universe, and not, as in Blackwood's novels, a wondering visitor to a world of plants and beasts.

But death intervened, and what he might have written can only be guessed from such poems as "The Song of Songs" and "Laus Deo" and "The Iron Age" in "The Cup of Comus." What he accomplished was worth doing, and he did it well. He put the meadows and forests of the South into poems as hauntingly beautiful as themselves.

FRANCIS THOMPSON

(1859-1907)

POETIC sensations are rare in our time. For a quarter of a century we have enjoyed a regular succession of excellent books of verse— verse graceful, fanciful, musical, interesting, and sometimes noble. Perhaps the general average of verse is higher to-day than it has previously been in the history of English letters. But there have been few books of verse which have caused the heart of the public to beat faster, few books of verse which critics have carried in their pockets for weeks at a time to show to their friends.

There has been one such book, however. In 1893 was published "Poems," by Francis Thompson. And this volume (as even Thompson's enemies cannot deny) excited, favorably or unfavorably, all its reviewers. Some hailed it as a work of surpassing genius, some found it irritatingly bad. But all felt about it passionately; no one damned it with faint praise and no one praised it with faint damns.

FRANCIS THOMPSON

Francis Thompson was a Roman Catholic and his faith gave him the themes, the imagery, often the phraseology, and the inspiration of all his best poetry. Yet his first most admiring critics were men by no means in sympathy with his religion. H. D. Traill, a North of Ireland Protestant, welcomed him as "a new poet of the first rank." Richard Le Gallienne called him "Crashaw born again, but born greater." John Davidson said "Thompson's poetry at its highest attains a sublimity unsurpassed by any other Victorian poet." And Arnold Bennett wrote of Thompson's second book "Sister Songs," "My belief is that Francis Thompson has a richer natural genius, a finer poetical equipment, than any poet save Shakespeare."

Of course there were hostile critics. Some of them were annoyed by the poet's phraseology, especially his use of words of Latin derivation and of forms which he coined for his own use. But most of them were annoyed by his themes; they resented the intrusion of a flaming Catholicity among the delicate artificial philosophies of the poets of the nineties, and their resentment found voice in attacks that recalled the brave old days of "This will never do" and "Back to your gallipots!" That this resentment continued, in some minds, even after the poet had died and his work had been received as an inalienable part of the world's treasury of English song is shown by the savagery of Austin Harrison's "review" of Everard Meynell's "Life of Francis Thompson" in the *English Review* in 1913.

Francis Thompson was born on the 16th of December, 1859, at Preston, Lancashire, England. In his boyhood he was taught at the school of the Nuns of the Cross and Passion, and in 1870 he entered Ushaw College. After seven years at Ushaw—years marked by one great tragedy, the decision by those in authority that his "nervous timidity" unfitted him for the priesthood—he went to Owens College as a student of medicine. His years in Manchester taught him little medicine, but they taught him other things destined to affect his life. Francis Thompson read books, but they were not surgical treatises. They were books of poetry, of essay, of theology, of scholastic philosophy. His love for music increased, and he attended more concerts than lectures. Also in Manchester he acquired his besetting sin—the opium habit. He took the drug first in the form of laudanum, during a painful illness. He continued to take it throughout many years of his life. It staved off the assaults of tuberculosis, it prevented his success in medicine or any other methodical and exact career, and thus removed what might have been rivals to the art of poetry. But, as his biographer says, opium "dealt with him remorselessly as it dealt with Coleridge and all its consumers. It put him in such constant strife with his own conscience that he had ever to hide himself from himself, and for conceal-ment he fled to that which made him ashamed, until it was as if a fig-leaf were of necessity plucked from the Tree of the Fall. It killed in him the capacity for acknowledging those duties to his family and friends, which, had his heart not been in shackles, he would have owned with no ordinary ardor."

Francis Thompson's years immediately after his failure in his medical examinations were spent in London, in poverty and ill health. But no man of genius can long remain hidden. In a strange and romantic manner, some of his magnificent poetry and prose came to the attention of Wilfred and Alice Meynell. They gave to the world the blessing of acquaintance with Francis Thompson's work, and to the poet they gave, in addition to more material benefits, the wise and affectionate friend-ship his lonely spirit most needed. He resisted the opium habit, increased in physical and mental health, gained congenial employment as a reviewer for the best of the London weeklies. The publication of his books established him, in the opinion of those whose opinion was most worth-while, as a figure of great literary importance. He died "a very good death" at the age of forty-eight. Had his mind been (as fortunately it was not) concerned with literature in his last hours he would have known that he had attained a fame of the kind that does not tarnish with the years, that he had realized the poet's ambition of adding substantially to the world's heritage of beauty.

If Francis Thompson is to be related by critics and historians of literature to writers of a more recent date than that of Crashaw and Southwell, it must be to the poets of the Pre-Raphaelite Brotherhood. What they promised, Thompson fulfilled. In a materialistic and sophisticated age, Rossetti and his friends sought to reproduce the romantic splendors of the Middle Ages. They took delight in the lovely externalities of the Catholic Church. Rossetti's friend, Coventry Patmore, went further than the Pre-Raphaelites; he became a Catholic and thus carried the theories of the Pre-Raphaelite Brotherhood to their logical and tremendous conclusion. Patmore's greater disciple,

FRANCIS THOMPSON

Francis Thompson, brought back to English poetry the knowledge, largely forgotten since the Reformation, that the proper study of mankind is God; he refused to limit his mind, as his contemporaries did theirs, by temporal and astronomical boundaries. A universal poet must sing the universe. And the center of the universe is God. So Francis Thompson sang of God, and in "The Hound of Heaven" he made of man's relation to God and God's relation to man a poem that is unsurpassed in the literature of spiritual experience. And all great poetry deals with spiritual experience.

JOHN MASEFIELD

(1874—)

TO be versatile and prolific generally is to be unimportant. Especially in literature, Jack-of-all-trades is, as a rule, master of none. An exception brilliantly proving this rule is John Masefield.

Homer (scholars tell us) was not one man but a company of poets, writing through more than one century. Shakespeare (we are encouraged to believe) was not a theatrical manager who liked occasionally to build a play to show his dramatists how it should be done, but a syndicate of philosophers, poets, playwrights, scientists, and politicians. Three hundred years from now literary detectives will busy themselves with discovering the names of the sailor, the farmer, the Hellenist, the Orientalist, the sociologist, the realist, the romanticist, the dramatist, the ballad maker, the sonneteer, the novelist, the short story writer, who called their conspiracy John Masefield. They will attribute some of the "Salt Water Ballads" to Kipling, some to Henry Newbolt, some to C. Fox Smith. They will attribute "The Sweeps of Ninety-Eight" to Dr. Douglas Hyde. They will attribute "The Faithful" to Sturge Moore. They will attribute "The Tragedy of Nan" to D. H. Lawrence, part of "A Mainsail Haul" to Charles Whibley, part of it to Algernon Blackwood, and part of it to Robert Louis Stevenson. And some of his ballads they will attribute to Wilfrid Gibson and some of his lyrics to William Butler Yeats. This will be a stupid thing for them to do, but nevertheless, they will do it.

One reason why the conduct of these hypothetical scholars is particularly irritating is that John Masefield is a writer of strong individuality. He has a distinct and easily recognizable style; his theme may be a battle of wits between Tiger Roche and the rebel hunters of 1798, or the tragedy of Nan Hardwick and the mutton parsties and the malicious Pargetters, or the great intrigues of royal Spain, or the ambitions of Pompey, or the soul of man in its relation to the mercy of God—whatever his theme may be, his style is the same. The writer's eyes may be fixed upon the mysteries of his own heart, or they may be searching the boundless heavens; he is, nevertheless, always a realist. They may be curiously studying the most ordinary details of modern life; he is, nevertheless, always an idealist. So the intellectual, perhaps it might be said the spiritual, attitude of John Masefield is unvarying. And in this is to be found the reason for the intense individuality of the writer as seen in his works, for the feeling, common to all his readers, of being in direct communication with him. And the style of the sequence of sonnets in the Shakespearean manner is much the same as that of the stories about pirates and the drama of ancient Japan. The nervous expressive diction, the direct Elizabethan colloquialism, these things are Masefield; the form may vary, but not in its characteristics, the language.

A writer's attitude toward life and toward the things beyond life is his own; it is not to be accounted for by heredity or environment. But a writer's style must necessarily be influenced by what he reads and by the talk of those with whom he spends the formative periods of his life. Even the careless reader of John Masefield's books will notice occasionally in them, especially in the lyrics, a strong Celtic flavor. Masefield's "Sea-Fever" and "Roadways" and "Cardigan Bay" and "Trade

Winds" and "The Harper's Song" surely belong to the same family as Eva Gore Booth's "The Little Waves of Breffny" and William Butler Yeats's "The Lake Isle of Innisfree." Furthermore, Masefield has that belief in the beauty of tragedy, tragedy in itself without regard to its moral significance, which is characteristic of many of the Irish writers of our generation. In the preface to "The Tragedy of Nan" he writes:

"Tragedy at its best is a vision of the heart of life. The heart of life can only be laid bare in the agony and exultation of dreadful acts. The vision of agony, or spiritual contest, pushed beyond the limits of the dying personality, is exalting and cleansing. It is only by such visions that a multitude can be brought to the passionate knowledge of things exulting and eternal. . . . Our playwrights have all the powers except that power of exaltation which comes from a delighted brooding on excessive, terrible things. That power is seldom granted to men; twice or thrice to a race perhaps, not oftener. But it seems to me certain that every effort, however humble, towards the achieving of that power helps the genius of a race to obtain it, though the obtaining may be fifty years after the strivers are dead."

Now in our time only one other writer has expressed this idea with equal force. And that writer is Mr. William Butler Yeats. He has written in an essay: "Tragic art, passionate art, . . . the confounder of understanding, moves us by setting us to reverie, by alluring us almost to the intensity of trance." So we find the Irish and the English writer guided by one impulse and by one conviction. And the result is that considering this, and considering also the Celtic idiom which seemingly comes so naturally from the lips of Mr. Masefield, Englishman though he be, in his lyrics, in his poetic dramas, and in many of the stories in "A Mainsail Haul," we are tempted to believe that the Irish literary movement has stretched a shadowy arm across the channel and laid its potent spell upon a man of Saxon blood. And to this theory Masefield's close friendship with William Butler Yeats lends color.

But there are flaws in this theory. One of them is that Masefield was writing in this manner before he met Yeats, before, indeed, the Irish literary movement had attracted much attention outside of its own home. Another flaw is, that this idea of the nobility, one might almost say, of the loveliness of tragedy, while it is in our time more Irish than

English, was held by the English dramatists and poets of centuries ago—Marlowe, for instance, and Webster and Shakespeare himself. The very earliest English poets selected tragic themes as a matter of course. Which of the great old ballads is without at least one bloody murder? Furthermore, the modern Irish-English idiom is to a great extent the idiom of England some centuries ago. There are rhymes in Shakespeare and even in Pope which show that what we consider Irish mispronunciations of English are simply English pronunciations that have been carried through the ages unchanged —the "ay" sound for "ea" is an example of that. "Our gracious Anne, whom the three realms obey, does sometimes counsel take, and sometimes tea." Chaucerian scholars say that the Wife of Bath talked what we would call Irish dialect. Now, John Masefield's literary idols belong not to his own generation or that immediately preceding it but to the early days of English letters. His favorite poem, he has told me, is Chaucer's "Ballad of Good Counsel." This reading has affected his style and it has affected also his thought, to the strengthening of the first and the deepening of the second.

There has been much said and written about

Masefield's romantic youth—about his experiences before the mast and behind the bar. There was a tendency during his tour of the United States in the early spring of 1916 to regard him as very much of a self-made man, to marvel at the miracle of genius which turned a bartender-sailor into a great poet. But the fact of the matter is that Masefield is essentially of the literary type, a man who might readily have supported himself by school-teaching, journalism, or some other unromantic trade, but deliberately selected colorful and exciting occupations. No one can talk to him and retain the idea that Masefield is a "sailor-poet" or a "bartender-poet." He is an educated English gentleman, very thoroughly a man of letters, who has had the good fortune to add to his treasury of experience by travels in strange places and among strange people.

Masefield's first important romantic experience, however, was undergone at a time when the poet was so young that it can scarcely have been the result of his own volition. Born in 1874 at Ledbury, in the west of England, he was indentured to a captain in the English merchant marine at the age of fourteen years. A fourteen-year-old boy on shipboard generally learns to hate passionately and consistently the sea and all that is associated with it. And it would not be strictly true to say that Masefield gained from this early adventure a love of the sea. Rather he then came under the spell of the sea, a spell from which he has never escaped. He has not that sentimental affection for the sea which inspires the life-on-the-ocean-waves' verse written by landsmen who know Neptune only by week-end visits in the summer time. He has been in the power of the sea more than it is altogether safe for so sensitive a spirit to be. He seems haunted by the sea; in those of his writings which in theme are least related to the sea the reader finds that again and again the figures and comparisons are drawn from the poet's memory of days when above and beyond him were nothing but water and sky. Not even Algernon Charles Swinburne was so much influenced by the sea as Masefield has been.

It is true that Masefield has given more beautiful expression to love for the sea than any other poet of our time—"Sea-Fever" alone would establish him as the sea's true lover. But also Masefield has expressed with terrible force the cruelty of the sea, its brutal and terrifying energy, its soul-shattering melancholy. And nowhere in English literature is it possible to find more vivid pictures of the bitter hardship of a seaman's life than in the "Salt Water Poems and Ballads." Masefield is not elective nor selective in his attitude toward the sea; his feeling toward the sea seems almost an obsession. The sea is not subject to his genius; it speaks through him.

Masefield's life on shipboard did more than put him in the power of the sea, it began his interest in the lives and thoughts of simple hard-working people. And this interest has never left him. It is true that he occasionally gives us something like "The Faithful" or "Philip, the King" or "The Tragedy of Pompey the Great." But his heart is in poems like "Dauber" and "The Everlasting Mercy" and in stories like "A Deal of Cards," in which he writes of unsophisticated people who feel strongly and do not conceal their emotions.

It was, perhaps, because of a real sense of the value and interest of life among simple people that Masefield made the selection he did of work to support himself during his first visit to the United States. In Connecticut he was a farm laborer, in Yonkers he was a hand in a carpet-factory and in New York City he was a sort of helper to the bartender in the old Colonial hotel on Sixth Avenue

near Jefferson Market Court. This hotel is still in
the possession of the family who employed Masefield and their recollections of him are highly entertaining. The writer once asked the eldest son of the
family if Masefield had written anything during the
days of his employment there. He had not, it
seemed, and he was associated in the minds of the
family with the art of poetry, for one reason only—
that being that he used to sing to the fretful baby,
holding it in his lap as he sat in a rocking-chair in
the kitchen, waiting for his employer's wife to serve
his dinner.

When Masefield went back to England he went
to work as a clerk in a London office. He was
writing now, putting on paper the pictures that
had been etched in his brain and in his heart during
his wander years. Now he perceived the deep and
abiding beauty and the deep and abiding tragedy
(to Masefield they were the same) of his experiences. How this knowledge came to him he has
told in twelve immensely sincere lines. E. A.
Robinson has said that poetry is a language which
tells, by means of a more or less emotional reaction,
that which cannot be stated in prose. And therefore it is better to let Masefield tell this in poetry

than to attempt to paraphrase it. He wrote, by way of preface to "A Mainsail Haul":

"I yarned with ancient shipmen beside the galley range,
And some were fond of women, but all were fond of change;
They sang their quavering chanties, all in a fo'c's'le drone,
And I was finally suited, if I had only known.

I rested in an ale-house that had a sanded floor,
Where seamen sat a-drinking and chalking up the score;
They yarned of ships and mermaids, of topsail sheets and slings,
But I was discontented; I looked for better things.

I heard a drunken fiddler in Billy Lee's saloon,
I brooked an empty belly with thinking of the tune;
I swung the doors disgusted as drunkards rose to dance,
And now I know the music was life and life's romance."

Masefield's work soon attracted the attention of William Butler Yeats, John Galsworthy, Sturge Moore, and other English men of letters, and largely through their efforts was brought to the attention of the public. American readers first became aware of him through the publication of two long poems—"The Everlasting Mercy" and "The Widow in the Bye Street." To say that these were long narrative, poems, dealing with intensely tragic and dramatic events in the life of the British poor, is not to describe them adequately. They were a poetry new to our generation. They showed an intimate knowledge of the lives of the poor, especially of the criminal poor, not to be found in the amiable poems of Mr. W. W. Gibson and similar socialistic dilettantes. They were not socialistic in message; rather they were individualistic. Saul Kane was not a drunkard because of economic pressure; Jimmy's siren lived an evil life merely because she was evil, not as a result of the injustice of man-made laws or anything else of the sort. So precedents were violated and Masefield scored a success of sensation. The savage colloquialisms of the poems, their violent emotionalism, their melodrama—these things brought them to the attention of a large number of people not ordinarily interested in the work of new poets, and thus an audience was prepared for the poet's later and more important work.

There can be no doubt that the work published

later was more important. There were crudities in these two narrative poems which seemed to be put there deliberately, in order to startle and shock the reader. Masefield followed these poems with other poems in the same manner done with much greater technical skill and with a more convincing sincerity. "Dauber" and "Biography" and the "Daffodil Fields" are more likely to be read by the next generation than are "The Widow in the Bye Street" and "The Everlasting Mercy," in spite of the fact that the last mentioned poem was awarded the Edward de Polignac prize of $500 by the Royal Society of Literature.

It is hard to tell just what form Masefield will finally select for the expression of his genius. He has written ballads, lyrics, plays, novels, short-stories, even histories, and all these forms he has molded to his own use. At the time of writing he is in France actively engaged in Red Cross work, and has begun to send to the magazines stories of the things that he has seen which entitle him to be called a great reporter. The quest for beauty has been and is his ruling passion—he is splendidly ex-plicit on this subject in the magnificent sequence of Shakespearean sonnets printed in "Good Friday and Other Poems." He has searched for this beauty on the boundless sea, in noisy barrooms, in English meadows, in the streets of New York. He is seeking it now, we may believe, in the tragedy and heroism of the battlefield. And always, his sonnets tell us, it is evasive and very distant, because its real dwelling place is his own soul.

WILLIAM VAUGHN MOODY

(1869-1910)

WILLIAM VAUGHN MOODY was throughout his life regarded as the most promising of the younger American poets. And when he died in 1810 most critics mourned for the unwritten lyrics and poetic dramas of which American literature had thus been robbed; they mentioned the author as a gifted youth, whom fate had removed at the beginning of a splendid career.

To a certain extent this attitude was a tribute to the youthful spirit of William Vaughn Moody, to his vivacity, energy and cheerfulness. But it was chiefly a new illustration of the fact that nowadays poets flower late in the season. Moody was forty-one years old when he died—and there was a time when the poet of forty was considered well past the meridian of his genius. Most of the great poets established their fame before they were thirty years old—Keats and Shelley died at twenty-five and twenty-nine respectively. But nowadays the poet of forty-five is still called young and the poet of thirty our kind critics consider a precocious infant.

As a matter of stern fact, it is doubtful that American literature has really lost much by Moody's death. He wrote "Gloucester Moors" and the "Ode in Time of Hesitation" and "The Faith Healer." The conscientious student of his work cannot escape the conviction that in these he gave the world all that he really had to give. Of course he would have written more—nature lyrics, poems on political and sociological questions, poetical dramas dealing with philosophical themes, prose plays of modern American life. But toward the end of his brief life his work was not gaining in force. Readers of "The Death of Eve" have little sorrow over the poet's failure to complete this play —the first two members of the trilogy which it was to conclude are nobly phrased, but they are so cloudy in thought and weak in dramatic construction that they do their author's fame little service. Prometheus, Pandora, Deucalion, Eve, Cain, Raphael, and Michael, angels and archangels, thrones, dominions and powers, were characters too mighty for the talent of this poet, who could handle adequately enough a problem of contemporary politics or draw quaint lessons from the caged beasts in a menagerie.

Perhaps the coldness which annoys some readers of Moody's poems, the sense of aloofness from the common experience of mankind, the artificiality which mars such expressions of sympathy for humanity as are intended in "Gloucester Moors," are things for which it is unjust to blame the poet. His friend, John M. Manly, wrote in the preface to his "Poems and Plays": "He was an epicure of life, a voluptuary of the whole range of physical, mental, and spiritual perfections." But in Moody's poetry we find more of the mind than of the heart; we feel that we are in the presence of a charming and cultured personality, but we have no feeling of intimacy with the writer.

"Of thine own tears thy song must tears beget," wrote Rossetti. "O singer, magic mirror hast thou none save thine own manifest heart." And a greater poet than Rossetti exclaimed, "Ah, must (Designer Infinite!) Thou char the wood ere thou canst limn with?" A similar thought was in Horace's mind when in the *Ars Poetica* he said, "if you wish me to week you must first weep yourself."

Well, few tears are drawn by Moody's poems, nor did many tears go into their making. His wood was not charred. But he was a conscientious and accomplished artist, doing the best he could with the powers that were his. His work is thoughtful, imaginative, and well-wrought, his "Great Divide" is destined to periodic revivals, and the best of his lyrics are sure of a place in the anthologies.

William Vaughn Moody was born in Spencer, Indiana, on July 8th, 1869. He was the son of a prosperous retired steamboat captain. In 1871 the family moved to New Albany, on the Ohio River. The elder Moody died in 1886. William Vaughn Moody went to Riverside Academy and entered Harvard in 1889, being then twenty years old. In his senior year he went abroad with a wealthy family as tutor to their son. During the trip he made a walking tour of the Black Forest and Switzerland with a party of friends, including Norman Hapgood. He also spent some time in Greece and Italy.

He returned to Harvard to study for his master's degree and stayed on as an instructor in English. In the autumn of 1895 he went to the University of Chicago as instructor in English, reaching the rank of assistant professor before his departure eight years later. His life at the University of Chicago seems to have been rather leisurely. It was varied by journeys abroad and bicycle tours in Illinois and

Wisconsin. Swimming, bicycling, golf, tennis, walking, and mountain-climbing are mentioned by Mr. Manly as Moody's favorite sports, and it is not to be wondered that he had little time for writing, however unexacting his academic duties may have been.

Although his connection with the University of Chicago did not cease until later, he taught no classes after 1902. He did, however, do a certain amount of work academic in character, editing some editions of the classics and collaborating with his friend Robert M. Lovett in a "History of English Literature." He first became known to the general public by the successful presentation of his prose play, "The Great Divide." He died in Colorado Springs on the seventeenth of October, 1910. A few months before his death he married Miss Harriet C. Brainerd.

It is interesting to trace the influences in Moody's work. He was very thoroughly a man of books, and some critics complain that there is more ink than blood in the veins of the people of whom he writes. Certainly it is possible to find traces of his reading on nearly every page that he wrote. The lovely fourth stanza of "Gloucester Moors" is Coleridge; "Faded Pictures" is Browning at his worst; and

WILLIAM VAUGHN MOODY

"The Daguerreotype" is a deliberate effort to imitate the irregular ode-form of Coventry Patmore. And of course "Heart's Wildflower" and "A Dialogue in Purgatory," like the lyrics in "The Masque of Judgment," are a Chicago version of Rossetti.

In his prose plays we find Moody writing with an energy which he seldom exhibited in his poetry. Not in Jerome K. Jerome's "The Passing of the Third Floor Back," nor in Charles Rann Kennedy's "The Servant in the House," is the idea of the beneficent effect of a powerful and virtuous nature more plausibly presented than in "The Faith Healer." And Moody obtained his effect more honestly than did Jerome and Kennedy; his faith-healer is merely a faith-healer to the end of the play, there is no suggestion that he is more than human. In many respects "The Faith Healer" is Moody's most important work. There is more poetry in its prose than in all his poetic dramas put together. When Michaelis makes love to Rhoda and tells the story of his childhood home, when Beeler describes the picture of Pan and the Pilgrim, and when Uncle Abe chants his prophecies and visions, then there is real poetry—poetry not unlike some of the best passages in Synge's plays. The "strange mounting sing-song" of Uncle Abe's speech evidently was the inspiration of the best parts of Mr. Ridgley Torrence's "The Rider of Dreams."

"The Great Divide" has been magnificently acted, but it is inferior in every respect to "The Faith Healer." Its theme—the contrast between the Puritan spirit which Moody considered typical of the Eastern States, and the generous paganism which he thought characteristically Western,— might be, and probably will be, the basis of an important play. But there never was a New Englander remotely resembling Ruth Jordan, there never was a Westerner remotely resembling Stephen Ghent. Hero and heroine, or villain and villainess, or whatever they are supposed to be, have actuality, it is true—the actuality of figures seen in a nightmare. And the other characters in the play have no actuality whatsoever. And the author's total lack of humor never injured his work more than in this play. It is painful to see situations essentially humorous made banal and dull by the author's obtuseness. If only the idea had occurred to Bernard Shaw instead of to William Vaughn Moody!

Perhaps one reason why "The Great Divide," convincing enough when well acted, is a lamentable thing on the printed page is because it is an attempt

to prove a theory. Moody was a Puritan, through
and through, and like all modern literary Puritans
he was desperately ashamed of his Puritanism. He
glorified what he thought to be the pagan ideal, and
in "The Great Divide" he wanted to show that the
large acceptances of Ghent were nobler than the
austere negations of Ruth. But paganism and
Puritanism are nothing but terms, almost meaningless from much repetition, and "The Great Divide"
is a play of terms, of symbols, of lay figures. And
the only things that it proves are Moody's total in-
ability to understand paganism and his reluctant
but inevitable sympathy with Puritanism.

It was his Puritanism that made Moody try to
stimulate the conscience of his land by means of
"An Ode in Time of Hesitation," his best sustained
long poem, and his most passionate utterance. It
was the Puritan who wrote "On a Soldier Fallen in
the Philippines." It was the Puritan who wrote
"The Brute." And I think that it was the Puritan
who wrote "Gloucester Moors." A pagan, such as
Moody desired to be, would not have worried about
the "souls distraught in the hold," nor would he have
worried over the fact that some of the crew had over-
eaten. Also, a pagan would have enjoyed the love-

liness of the wild geranium and the barberry without asking:

> "Who has given to me this sweet,
> And given my brother dust to eat?
> And when will his wage come in?"

These things are manifestations of that Puritan characteristic known as "the New England conscience"—the cause in recent years of many rather frantic efforts at social and economic and philosophical readjustment. Mr. John M. Manly says that "Gloucester Moors" is "a favorite poem with workers in the slums,"—a significant and startling observation.

Moody's Puritanism gives strength to many of his poems, but in others it produces strange inconsistencies and evasions. It helped him to write "The Brute"—a strong and sincere poem. But it caused him to fail ridiculously in "A Dialogue in Purgatory," in "Good-Friday Night," and in "Song Flower and Poppy." In the second half of the last-named poem we come upon the root of the matter—Moody's complete failure to understand any religious system, any philosophy of life, more warm and comprehensive than his own Puritanism. He rebelled against this Puritanism, yet he could not escape it. He sought vaguely after paganism, whereas he could no more have been a Bacchic reveller than he could have been a Druid. In spite of his reading of early French and Italian romances, he failed utterly to see the generous glories of the Middle Ages, when all that was noble and beautiful in paganism was made a part of the richest civilization the world has yet known. He thought of intellectual development and spiritual freedom as things beginning about 1517—and naturally this hampered him when he wrote about Michael, Raphael, Azaziel, Eve, Jubal, and Cain.

A longer residence in Italy might have given him a more liberal culture and a spiritual philosophy generous without being pagan, pure without being Puritanical. And therefore the critics who said that a poet of promise died in 1910 may have told the truth. A broader culture and more extensive human sympathies would have enabled this deft artist in words to give to the world a message of the kind it always welcomes—to express beautifully the beauty that is truth.